Up the Ladder: Accessing Grades 3–6 Information Units of Study

Lucy Calkins, Hareem Atif Khan, and Shana Frazin

Photography by Peter Cunningham

Illustrations by Kimberly Fox

HEINEMANN ◆ PORTSMOUTH, NH

This book is dedicated to Kathleen Tolan. May her memory inform and influence our work with teachers and children. Forever.

Heinemann
361 Hanover Street
Portsmouth, NH 03801–3912
www.heinemann.com

Offices and agents throughout the world

The authors and publisher wish to thank those who have generously given permission to reprint borrowed material:

Passages from *A Beginner's Guide to Electricity and Magnetism*, Copyright © Gill Arbuthnott, 2016, A&C Black Children's & Educational, an imprint of Bloomsbury Publishing Plc.

Excerpt from *Oh Rats!: The Story of Rats and People* by Albert Marrin, copyright © 2006 by Albert Marrin. Used by permission of Dutton Children's Books, an imprint of Penguin Young Readers Group, a division of Penguin Random House LLC. All rights reserved.

Passages from *A Seed is Sleepy* © 2007 by Dianna Hutts Aston, illustrated by Sylvia Long. Used with permission of Chronicle Books LLC, San Francisco. Visit ChronicleBooks.com.

"Skunks" by Sandra Markle. Text copyright © 2007 by Sandra Markle. Reprinted with permission of Lerner Publishing Group, a division of Lerner Publishing Group, Inc. All rights reserved. No part of this text excerpt may be used or reproduced in any manner whatsoever without the prior written permission of Lerner Publishing Group, Inc.

Cataloging-in-Publication data is on file with the Library of Congress.

ISBN-13: 978-0-325-09656-8

Editors: Karen Kawaguchi and Tracy Wells
Production: Elizabeth Valway
Cover and interior designs: Jenny Jensen Greenleaf
Photography: Peter Cunningham
Illustrations: Kimberly Fox
Composition: Publishers' Design and Production Services, Inc.
Manufacturing: Steve Bernier

Printed in the United States of America on acid-free paper
21   20   PAH   4   5

Contents

BEND III   Taking Your Writing from Good to Great

Registration instructions to access the digital resources that accompany this book may be found on the inside back cover.

Acknowledgments

THIS UNIT will never stop being written. This is because the questions that guide it never grow old. How do we make information writing accessible and exciting in the way that story-telling seems to be? How do we simplify our best teaching of structure and organization? How do we inspire children to write with volume, voice, and verve?

At the Teachers College Reading and Writing Project, we ask these questions afresh as we pore over children's writing collected from classrooms in Pakistan and Jordan and Israel, as we study the writing done by children across New York City, Texas, Wisconsin, and Ohio. We turn to colleagues and friends at the Project and drink in their latest work, rethinking, prodding, re-imagining, and then tentatively drafting bends and teaching points to pilot. "Keep it simple," we remind each other. And we all return to the drawing board to revise, yet again.

Colleen Cruz was one of the first people we turned to. "How do you make this easier for children? For teachers?" she pushed. Then of course, with characteristic deftness, Colleen provided some answers that directed our baby draft at its very onset. Melissa Stewart ruminated with us over the telephone. The ambidextrous Julia Mooney tamed our unruliest drafts, whipped up the words that eluded us, and reread each draft with an unforgiving eye. Katie Clements decluttered our initial bend, setting a standard for the bends that followed. Kelly Boland Hohne brought her brilliance and bootcamp work ethic to our effort, thinking through several possibilities for how this unit could have gone. Valerie Geschwind, fingers flying over her keyboard, helped us draft at moments when energy was low. Jamie Wang stepped forward to scan, chart, and organize. Kimberley Fox thoughtfully read through each session and found a way to bring each chart to life with quirky icons.

Thank you to Elizabeth Franco, LaKisha Howell, Jonathan Aldanese, and Whitney Millichap for working on session videos and to Timothy Lopez for his patience and humor when the lights and camera stopped cooperating.

We are so grateful to the teachers who piloted this unit. You'll catch glimpses of their students' writing across this book. Of course we wrote this unit with the intention that children would write a lot, but nothing had prepared us for the volume and spunkiness of the writing we received from the classrooms of Amy Parisi, Debbie Ireland, Josh Richter, Danielle Apellaniz, Rebecca Migiano, Nicholle Bingham, Jill Teplica, Mary Ellen Robertson, and Janet Sayegh. We are grateful to coaches Amy Cabral and Bonnie Caton and to administrators Christine Press, Lenny Cerlich, Sharon Epple, Helena Nitowski, and Robin Young. Above all, we are full of wonder at the expertise with which the writers in their classrooms have educated us on cat grooming, minecraft, origami, packing for a road trip, dancing, and other equally compelling topics. If there was ever a doubt that our youngsters are capable teachers on topics about which adults have little clue, their writing has put them firmly to rest.

Thanks to the entire production team at Heinemann, particularly Karen Kawaguchi, Tracy Wells, and Elizabeth Valway. Abby Heim has painstakingly overseen every stage of the process, advising, cheering, and being ever-patient with re-drafts and deadlines. We couldn't have done this without her.

Writing Lots of Books that Teach

Bend I: Writing Lots of Books that Teach

This unit has been written for upper-grade students who have not received a lot of instruction in the kind of writing that falls under the umbrella of information/nonfiction writing. The unit provides them with lots of opportunities to write information texts on topics of personal expertise. The unit helps them envision the larger topic of an information text as being comprised of smaller subtopics, and to write about each of those subtopics separately, bucketing them. Students are given repeated opportunities to practice doing this work and a handful of planning and revision strategies to help them. They also learn to write with concrete, specific information and to elaborate, saying more about kernels of information. The goal of the unit is to accelerate students' growth in this genre while also helping them to build their identities as writers, their volume of writing. Above all, the unit aims to help youngsters learn to love writing.

You could teach this as your very first writing workshop unit, but it has actually been written with the assumption that you already launched the writing workshop in a narrative unit. If the decision is made that you'll bypass narrative work, you'll need to do a little back-peddling because this unit begins with the assumption that students have already learned some of the routines and structures of writing workshop. They sit with another student in the minilessons and that other person is their partner. Usually partnerships last for the duration of a unit, if not longer. This structure is very helpful to youngsters, and it is even helpful to name one person in each partnership as "Partner 1" and one as "Partner 2" so that you can suggest that when kids turn and talk during the minilesson, sometimes Partner 1 takes the lead, and sometimes Partner 2 does. That way the same child doesn't dominate repeatedly.

You'll find the *Guide to the Writing Workshop* contains many tips such as that one. That book can give you a super-quick crash course in managing a writing workshop and in the major methods that you use repeatedly when teaching writing. It is more to read—but it'll help a lot.

Our hope is that if you did launch your students with the narrative Up the Ladder unit, by now, your students will be more able to carry on as writers during writing time, and you will be finding it easier to confer and lead small groups. Aim to lead at least one small group and a few conferences every day. The kids don't need exhaustive one-to-one instruction, but they really profit from quick coaching. There are tips within each session on small groups that you will want to lead that day and conferences that will be especially helpful. Really, the content of those sections of this book pertains to every other day. Ideally, you will compile a repertoire of conferring and small-group ideas and draw on them in response to what you see your youngsters doing.

We encourage you to regard a session as a day. If the unit suggests that your kids will write a table of contents in a day, but your kids want to write with really beautiful fonts and to list twelve chapter titles, thereby taking two days on just the table of contents, we suggest you revisit. Perhaps they'll want to bring that work home to complete, because in class, they'll have new work to do tomorrow. And the truth is, a table of contents that is dashed down quickly and lists five chapters will work better anyhow! And that tip relates not only to the day in which kids write their tables of contents, but to every day.

You'll see that this bend invites kids to essentially write an information book on Days One, Three, and Five and to revise those books on Days Two, Four, and Six. That may seem awfully ambitious to you, but remember that the goal of the unit is for kids to be given lots and lots of opportunities for repeated independent practice, not to produce perfect pieces. You'll teach kids how to choose a topic, to plan their book, and to write it. During the first bend, it will be important for you to channel writers to write in booklets that give them ambitious but realistic goals.

You enter this unit knowing about the volume of writing your writers produce in one sitting. Use this data to inform what paper you guide students toward. That is, if students currently fill a sheet of lined notebook paper in one sitting, then you will want to guide those students toward paper with lots of lines. It is important to remember they'll be drafting books of four to six pages in a day. If you think, however, that your writers can only write a few small paragraphs in a day's writing time, then give them booklets full of paper that is just a bit beyond those expectations.

Of course, your expectations will differ based on the specific child, so plan on having three or four different sorts of booklets in play, and on moving kids from a less to a more advanced booklet between the start and the end of Bend I. You will find a variety of templates for paper choices to support your writers in the online resources.

The major work that you are inviting kids to do is to take a topic they know about and to use information writing as a way to teach others about that topic. For now, you aren't worrying about their writing having a lead that hooks readers, or an ending that wraps things up, or anything else. Your goal is for writers to write fluently, and to feel as if they are teaching on the page. You also hope they put one thing (one subtopic) on each page.

As soon as writers have books drafted, you'll begin to lift their knowledge of good information writing. You'll teach writers that they can revise their writing to add on to it, and that one way to do that is to ask the sorts of questions that readers might ask: Who? What? Where? Why? Later you'll teach writers that information books are comprised of information, and that concrete, particular information matters. You'll encourage them to write with names, numbers, quotes, and details.

Of course, part of this will involve supporting revision. You will want to see students going back to add more details to their pieces, either to their drawings or their words or both. Your students will revise in concrete manipulative ways through the use of revision strips, giant Post-its, and flaps stuck off the edges of a page.

You'll teach students to search for and eliminate run-on sentences. Run-ons are a predictable outgrowth of elaboration. As you teach kids to write more about their topics, they will invariably do this by using "Scotch-tape" words like *and*, *so*, and *then*. You'll also want your students to apply the editing work they've learned in previous units. You'll create a "New and Improved Editing Checklist" that channels kids to continue to use all they know to make their writing presentable while adding this new skill of editing for run-ons into the mix.

By the end of the bend, your students' folders should be stuffed with several completed books—and you will also want to see evidence that these pieces have been revised. A word to the wise: Don't feel that your kids need to recopy their books, fixing every error, prior to publication. In this unit, we are suggesting three bends, which means three celebrations. You probably don't want to stop your kids' forward progress by having them devote a day (and we know it generally turns into several days) to the slow work of recopying their rough-draft writing.

You will notice that this bend ends with a small celebration. You may decide to create a splashier one. Celebrations matter. They provide an opportunity for your students to glory in their progress. Reveling in your students' writing will help them develop identities as writers and will rally enthusiasm for the work to come in Bend II.

A Vision for Growth

Bend I–Volume: Children will write three quick books.

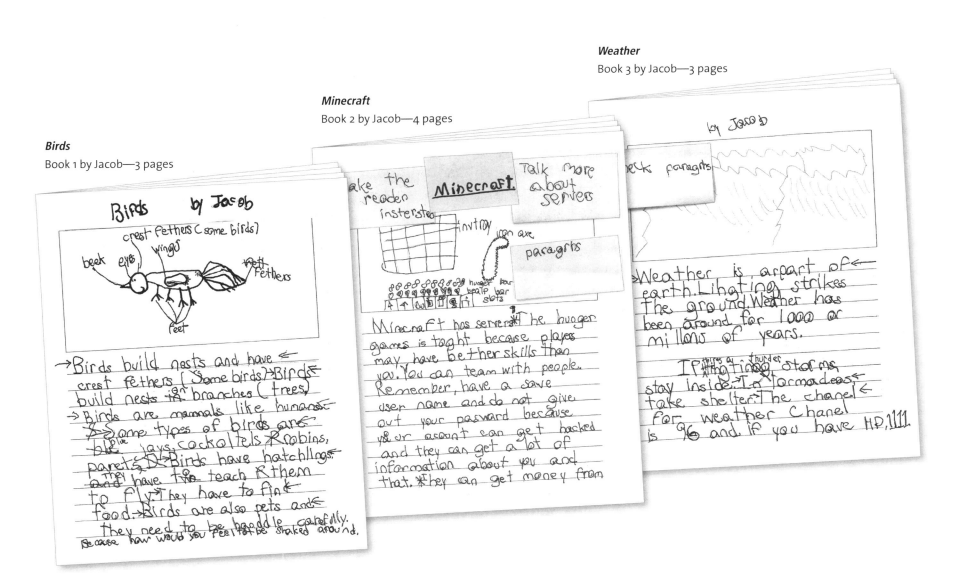

Weather
Book 3 by Jacob—3 pages

Minecraft
Book 2 by Jacob—4 pages

Birds
Book 1 by Jacob—3 pages

Bend II–Organization: Children will organize 1–2 books into chapters.

Soccer
Book 5 by Jacob—15 pages

All About Jacob
Book 4 by Jacob—9 pages

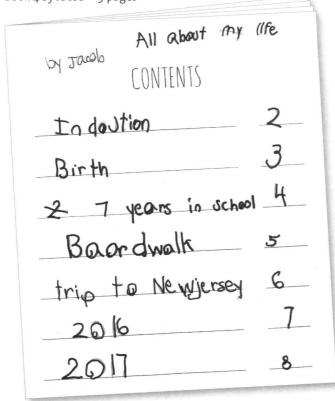

All about my life

by Jacob

CONTENTS

In dovtion _____ 2

Birth _____ 3

2 7 years in school 4

Baordwalk _____ 5

trip to New jersey 6

2016 _____ 7

2017 _____ 8

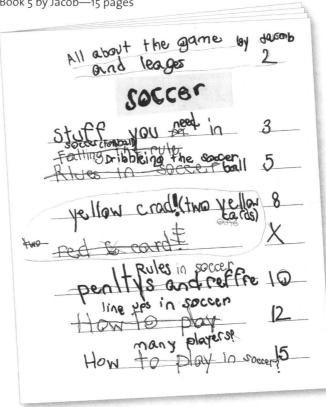

All about the game by Jacob
and leages 2

soccer

stuff you need in 3
soccer
Fatting Dribbking the soccer
Rlues in soccer ball 5

yellow crad!(two yellow 8
cards)
two red card X

Rules in soccer
penltys and reffre 10
line ups in soccer
How to play 12
many players!
How to play in soccer 15

Writers Write to Teach

IN THIS SESSION

TODAY YOU'LL teach students that writers plan information books much like they plan true stories. They think of a topic, touch and tell a page, sketch what they'll write, write that page, and then repeat the process with the next page.

TODAY STUDENTS will write their first information book. Expect to see them writing about their topic across multiple pages.

GETTING READY

✓ Before this session, be sure to stock your writing center with blank booklets. We recommend your booklets be four to six pages. The number of lines per page will differ based on your expectation for each writer; you are expecting writers to complete a booklet a day.

✓ Pair students with writing partners, and ask them to sit in the meeting area next to their writing partner. This will happen every day (see Connection).

✓ Display the "How to Write an Information Book" anchor chart (see Teaching).

✓ Choose a topic and prepare to model how to plan an information book. We model with "All about Fireworks" (see Teaching).

✓ Make a giant booklet out of chart paper to demonstrate for students how you plan (see Teaching).

✓ Prepare to distribute blank booklets to students, and add additional blank pages to students' tables (see Active Engagement and Link).

✓ Print small copies of "Topics for Information Writing" for students in small groups (see Conferring and Small-Group Work).

✓ Clear out students' writing folders from the earlier narrative unit, or if you did not teach that unit, prepare a writing folder for each student, with a red dot on one pocket for work that is stopped and a green dot on the other pocket for work that is still underway (see Share).

✓ Scan the QR code to view the brief video to get a vision for how the work in this minilesson might sound. There is a video available for every minilesson.

hein.pub/UTLINFO_1

✓ Review tips for additional support when working with English as a New Language (ENL) students at the end of this and every session.

Writers Write to Teach

CONNECTION

Rally students to a new unit on information writing by helping them realize they can be powerful teachers on topics they know a lot about.

"Writers, we haven't been together that long, but I'm already realizing something about you. I thought *I* was the teacher in this room, but I'm coming to realize . . ." I dropped my voice to a whisper. "Sometimes *I'm the student*. It's the truth. When you talk about things like Nerf guns or creating your own apps, I realize that I'm *not* the only teacher in this room. On a million topics, you are my teachers."

If a student or two do not have a topic, you can suggest topics that you know almost any student could write about—the school, the playground, the mall.

Model how to generate topics on which you are an expert. Give partnerships time to share topics they know a lot about.

"Think for a second about a topic on which you're an expert, one that you could teach others." I left a moment for silence. "Are you thinking of things you do often? Things you love? A place you visit a lot?"

"I'll start. Hmm, . . . What's something I do a lot or love? I know! Every July, I love watching the fireworks. So I could teach 'fireworks.' What about you? Think of one topic, for now, any one. Ready to whisper your topic to your partner?" I waited a sec to let momentum build, then said, "Go!"

If you examine the details of this transcript, you'll get a sense for the ways in which your pacing can create momentum and energy. Trust the power of silences that give kids a half-moment to think, and of urgent quick commands—Go!—that mobilize kids quickly. Become skilled at reconvening kids' attention.

After children shared for twenty seconds, I reconvened them, saying, "This month in our writing workshop, you'll be doing information writing, nonfiction writing. You'll write lots of books in which you teach readers all about a topic. But you can't just pick up the pen and begin scribbling in your book. Your information would be all jumbled! Instead, you need to plan."

❧ Name the teaching point.

"Today I want to teach you that before writers write an information book, they plan how their book will go. You plan your book by thinking of a topic, touching and telling a page, quickly sketching what you'll write on that page, and then writing. Then you repeat that on each new page."

When delivering this teaching point—and any teaching point—don't hesitate to look down at the page of the book a little as you talk, gathering the words into your mind and then saying them—so it sounds like talk, not read-aloud, yet you stay close to the actual transcript. Usually, it works best to stay close to the wording in the book, as that wording is woven into anchor charts and future sessions.

TEACHING

Connect the work students do to write true stories about their lives to the work that information writers do as they write teaching books: think, touch and tell, sketch, and write.

"Do you remember how you learned that when writers are writing stories, it helps to think of an idea, then touch and tell the story across pages, then sketch the story and then write? Well, now that you're writing teaching books, I made a few little changes to the 'How to Write a True Story' chart so that it matches this new type of writing you will be doing." I revealed a new chart.

> **ANCHOR CHART**
>
> ### How to Write an Information Book
>
> 1. **Think** of something you could teach.
>   Things you do?
>   Places you visit?
>   Sports you play?
>   People you admire?
> 2. **Touch** a page, **tell** the part of your topic you plan to teach on that page, and **sketch** the things you'll write about.
>   Say the actual words you might write.
> 3. **Write that one page.**
>   On each page, just write about the one part of your topic you plan for that page.
> 4. **Touch and tell and sketch** the next page, then write it . . .
>   and so on through your book.

Recruit kids to join you as you plan for your information book.

"Will you notice whether I do each of these things as I plan my information book?" I shifted into the role of writer, holding up a giant chart-sized book. "I decided my topic would be fireworks," I said, glancing up at the chart. "To get started, I'll touch the page and tell the parts of my topic I'll teach on the first page." I touched the first page. "Let's see. On the first page I could teach you about kinds of fireworks. Could you help me come up with things to teach related to that?" A buzz of talk began.

The planning process you are teaching differs in this unit from that which your students used in the narrative unit. When writing information books, we recommend students sketch then write one page at a time. Narrative writing has a coherence and unity from beginning to end that requires an overarching plan. Information writing, on the other hand, is composed of a number of subtopics—discrete chunks of content. Young writers often deal with their subtopics one at a time.

After a few seconds, I reconvened the class. "You've given me awesome help. You are right that I can teach about sparklers on this page, and about the kind of fireworks that burst into flower shapes in the sky." I started drawing a sparkler—and muttered quietly, as if I were thinking aloud to myself, "They are pretty simple, just a sparkle at the end of a stick." After drawing a sparkler, I quickly sketched a firecracker that bursts into flower shapes and floats down. I then made a rocket that shoots up in a tight spiral, and said, "I'm ready to write now. I'm going to tell about the sparkler first—it is the simplest—then the flower, then the spiral." I added numbers alongside each.

I picked up a marker and wrote, "Sparklers are the simplest kind of fireworks. They are just a stick . . ."

Then I paused, and said, "When I finish writing *all* I know about kinds of fireworks on this page, I'll go to this next page. Maybe then I'll teach people that fireworks are dangerous."

Debrief your modeling so it feels replicable to your students.

"Are you noticing the steps we've used so far?" I gestured toward chart. "First, we thought of a topic, then we touched and told a page, and then quickly sketched what we'll write on that page. Now, we're ready to write long before we move to the next page."

ACTIVE ENGAGEMENT

Channel students to plan the sections of their information book with their partner.

"Are you ready to try this planning with your own topic?" I passed around blank booklets.

"Will either you or your partner pick up your booklet, touch the pages, and tell in just a word, what you're going to write on each page? Then go back to page one and say *all* that you'll write on that one page. As your partner talks, lean in and listen and even . . . guess what . . . ask questions!"

As kids broke into a buzz, teaching each other, I circulated among them, leaning in and nodding encouragement, occasionally prompting and coaching:

- "Say the exact words you'll write on that page."

- "It sounds like you just moved to a new thing about your topic. That would go on the *next* page. Stay with this topic on this page."

- "Lean in as your partner talks. Listen in a way that helps your partner say more."

After a minute, I said, "Cia realized she was starting to teach about a new part of her topic, and so you know what she did? She turned the page so the new information went on its own page! Well done!"

Teachers, it's okay that children get started and do not completely finish this, and it is definitely okay that there is not enough time for all partners to exchange roles. Your goal is to teach writers that this sort of planning helps, not to make sure each writer leaves the minilesson with a fully planned book.

LINK

Remind students that planning is an integral part of information writing. One way that writers plan is by thinking of a topic, touching and telling, sketching, and then writing.

"Writers, in a minute you'll grab your pens and get to work writing up a storm. I left lots of blank pages in the middle of your tables in case you need to add to your book. Before you start," I gestured toward our chart and read off, "remember that you need to . . . think of a topic, touch and tell what you'll teach across the pages, sketch out what you'll teach, and then you write. Off you go to sketch and write!"

It may seem counterintuitive to interrupt the turn-and-talk this quickly, rather than waiting for kids to exhaust all they have to say. In fact, calling back children's attention when the momentum of conversation is at a high level actually maintains the minilesson's energy and engagement.

FIG. 1–1   This writer is a *Star Trek* fan!

Keep Energy and Productivity High

TODAY, expect your kids will each write an entire nonfiction book. For that to be possible, make sure there are a limited number of lines on each page and a limited number of pages in the booklets you give to kids. It is far better for kids to come close to filling their pages, than for them to write on three out of twenty lines! The texts your kids are writing today are more like nonfiction picture books than chapter books—you'll see that the unit progresses toward chapter books, and it is best to avoid stealing the thunder from upcoming sessions.

During this bend, kids will write about a book a day, every other day, alternating with days for revision. Today you can expect that kids will probably smush stuff on several subtopics onto some of their pages, so you can begin immediately to teach them categorization—the concept of bucketing their information so like-information is slotted together. Don't, however, teach them to label each page as a different chapter. (That is the work of Bend II).

Your main goal is to encourage kids to write up a storm, writing in a way that is different from their narratives. Encourage kids to write on topics that they may not have originally thought were interesting to others: sugary cereals, or the tricks that goalies use to protect the goal, or the traditions connected to the religious faith practiced by their families.

Because this is Day One of a new unit, you will probably not hold three-minute conferences with individuals. Instead, you may decide to circle the room, whispering in quick compliments and directions, making sure to keep your own volume low and their productivity high:

- *Give a thumbs up to a writer who seems to be staring into space.* "I can tell you're planning. Put it all down. Get started." Gently tap the paper and move away.

- *To a student who's dawdling.* "Are you giving that hand a rest? Let me see you flex those writing fingers. Great . . . pick up that pen."

- "It looks like you're writing a *story* about one moment you spent at the Yankees game. Remember this month you'll write information books in which you'll teach the reader. Decide: do you want to teach readers about the game of baseball or about the team, the Yankees?"

- "It looks like you are putting everything about your topic on this first page. How might you divide up all this information so that it goes across pages? Walk me through the pages."

- "You've got some spectacular sketches there. Can you touch each sketch and teach me as much as you can about that one sketch, then we'll go to the next?" Midway through this: "I gotta stop you. You've got to put this down."

MID-WORKSHOP TEACHING Writers Reread to Add More Information by Asking, "What Else Can I Teach?"

"Writers, eyes on me." When I had their attention, I said, "You're off to a solid start. I see many pens flying—but sometimes, I see kids stopping, staring off into the distance. Here's a tip for when you feel stuck. Ask yourself, 'What else can I teach?' Don't forget that you're an expert on your topic! You know a lot. Push yourself to put all that information onto the page. Get back to writing!"

If some students have trouble generating topic ideas, then pull a quick small group.

To get ready, print the chart "Topics for Information Writing." Have students bring their blank booklets to the rug. Set them up to work as partners. Tell the children why you gathered them for this small group: "Writers, I've gathered you because sometimes, when writers get stuck around topic choice, they reach out and talk to friends to jog their thinking." Then, coach partners to use the chart to help each other generate some topics and to pick one. When a writer tentatively says, "Well, I could maybe write on . . .," encourage partners to get behind that topic, endorsing it. "Yes! That'd be so great!" Once partners have topics, encourage them to open books and teach each other about their topic, touching each page as they rehearse.

Writers Organize Ongoing and Finished Work

Set students up to organize their work, and then to tell a nearby kid what they learned about the difference between information books and stories.

"Writers, notice that I'm putting a box of your cleaned-out folders from the narrative unit onto each of your tables. Find your folder—it is now for your information writing—and put your book in it. Most of you have finished your book. If so, put it in the red dot side of your folder. If you still have a tiny bit of work to do before your book is done, where do you put the book?"

The kids chimed that it goes under the green dot, and I nodded. "As you do that, tell someone near you what you learned today about how information books are different than stories. Go!"

WORKING WITH ENL STUDENTS

This session is already very supportive for ENLs:

◆ The process for writing an information book provides clear, actionable, and transferable steps (see "How to Write an Information Book" chart).

◆ The class book begun by the teacher and then continued by the students provides support for language, as well as learning the writing process. In particular, sketching images before writing can give every writer access.

◆ Oral rehearsal during the minilesson supports writers in listening and speaking the language of information writing.

To provide additional support for ENLs, you might:

◆ Use lots of gestures and an animated voice when referring to the steps on the "How to Write an Information Book" chart. Connect each action to a step on the chart.

◆ Encourage students who are doing lots of sketching to label their sketches. If necessary provide sentence starters like "This is a . . ." and "It is . . ."

◆ Allot additional time for students to orally rehearse their pages before they write.

Elaboration

Writers Ask "Who, What, Where, Why" Questions

IN THIS SESSION

TODAY YOU'LL teach students that information writers work to teach readers something new and interesting on each page. They return to their draft, asking "Who, What, Where, Why" questions, and then answering them by adding more information to each page.

TODAY STUDENTS will revise their first information books in *big* ways. Expect to see them thinking of new information they can teach on each page and then taping strips of paper or putting large Post-its onto the pages of their books where they can write the new information.

GETTING READY

✔ Mark up the class book from the previous session with Post-it feedback from another teacher (see Connection).

✔ Ask students to bring their writing folder and pencil or pen to the meeting area. Do thie every day (see Active Engagement).

✔ Display the "How to Write an Information Book" anchor chart. Do this every day (see Teaching Point).

✔ Prepare a "Writers Ask Questions" one-day chart (see Teaching).

✔ Add revision strips, flaps, Post-its, and loose pages to each table (see Conferring and Small-Group Work).

✔ Print out copies of "Breakfast" for small groups (see Conferring and Small-Group Work).

✔ Today's minilesson video:

hein.pub/UTLINFO_2

Elaboration

Writers Ask "Who, What, Where, Why" Questions

CONNECTION

Rally your students to the idea that they'll be revising today by suggesting that yesterday's information books feel too empty. Suggest it will be important to add a lot to them.

"Writers, when you come to the meeting area, please bring your writing folder with the information book you wrote yesterday and sit on it," I said, and then waited until the class had assembled on the carpet. "Yesterday, we wrote an information book about fireworks. I was proud of it, so I gave it to Ms. North to read. She left some feedback Post-its. I haven't had a chance to peek at them. Should we?" I opened the book, and made a show of delighting in the Post-it feedback left throughout.

I highlighted one piece of feedback. "Look, on my first page about the types of fireworks, Ms. North wrote, 'Wow!' I bet she was surprised about our information.

"And here," I pointed to a Post-it. "She wrote, '*More!*' I guess she wants to know more about the dangers of firecrackers. That's helpful feedback!" I flipped the page to reveal another Post-it, and the kids could see I was a bit surprised to see this one, again, contained the message '*More!*'" I looked up, struck by realization. "I guess this book felt too empty to her. I need to fix this. I should add much more information to each page."

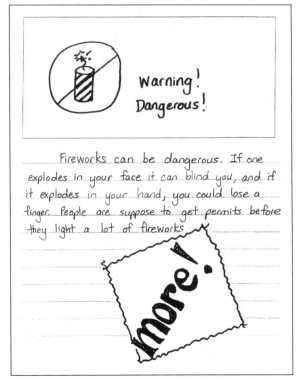

FIG. 2–1

Name the teaching point.

"Today I want to teach you that to write information books that teach the reader something new and interesting, it helps to return to a draft, adding more information to each page." I added to our chart.

TEACHING

Recruit the class to ask "Who, What, Where, Why" questions and then answer these, as a way to generate ideas for more information to put on each page.

"Let's look at this second page.

> Fireworks can be dangerous. If not handled with care they might cause serious injury.

"I agree with my reader. This page really does look skimpy. I'll need your help to add more. Right now, would you turn to your partner and use one of these question words to ask a question?" I uncovered a chart with "who, what, where, and why" bullet points.

As kids began to talk, I used that time to quickly chart out the following questions, pausing midway to voice over: "Writers, I hear some 'Who' questions and some 'Why' questions. Try now to generate some 'Where' questions too." I quickly jotted questions as students turned and talked.

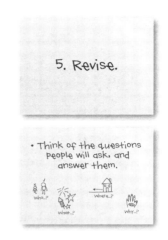

Your kids may not actually ask these questions. You can alter them to match what your kids say, or you can just pretend these are the question you heard. The goal here is to get some questions down quickly so they grasp the concept of using these key words to generate questions. Just record a few of the questions and say the others.

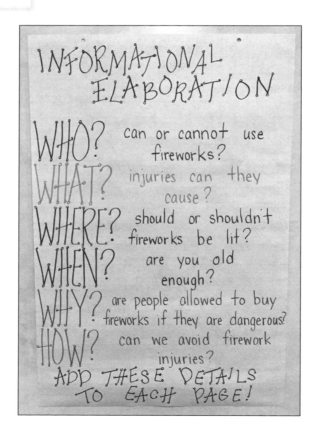

I called the class's attention to the chart. "You've helped me come up with a goldmine of questions! These'll help me add so much more to this page. I pointed to the third question, read it, "*Where* should and shouldn't fireworks be lit?" and thought about the answer. "Tell your partners what we could add to this page as an answer to that question."

As the room buzzed, I turned to the book and added to the page:

> Fireworks can be dangerous. If one explodes in your face it can blind you, and if it explodes in your hand, you could lose a finger. People are supposed to get permits before they light a lot of fireworks. Fireworks should only be lit in places where there is a lot of space. You shouldn't light fireworks in a big crowd of people. That would be dangerous!

I convened children's attention. "See how one question helped us create more sentences of information! We could do the same with the rest of these questions."

Debrief in a way that helps this work feel replicable to students.

"First, a writer rereads a skimpy page and uses the prompts 'Who, What, Where, Why' to create possible questions. Then you answer one of the questions by adding information to your skimpy page. Then you take on another question."

ACTIVE ENGAGEMENT

Set partners up to ask "Who, What, Where, Why" questions from a chosen page in their information book as a way to say more on that page.

"In a minute, you'll have the chance to help each other do this work. But first, open up to a page in your information book that looks a little empty." I allowed thirty seconds before adding: "With the help of your partner, brainstorm some 'Who, What, Where, Why' questions that could be asked on that page. You don't have to answer these questions just yet. Focus first on simply coming up with useful questions."

I circulated as much as the space around the rug would allow, listening in and coaching as partners helped each other generate questions with prompts such as:

- "Don't rush to answer the questions just yet. That comes later. Generate another question . . ."

- "Remind your partner to only ask questions that fit what *this* page is about."

- "I hear some 'Who' questions. Vary it up. Are there 'What' and 'Why' questions you might ask?"

- "Don't let your partner off the hook! Ask your partner to suggest possible questions also. This is partner work, not solo work."

This is more writing than you can do quickly if you are writing on chart paper. One tip is to just draw your pen across the page and say aloud the words you'll later write. Another option is to scrawl them on your clipboard (or pretend to do so), displaying them later.

Students will feel an urgency to answer a question the minute it is raised. But you want to teach them to hold off on the answers just now, instead focusing their energy on simply articulating multiple questions. Learning starts with questions, not answers.

I leaned in to listen, allowing just a minute for partners to generate questions. Then, convening students' attention, I called for a quick share. "I heard some fantastic questions circulating the room. Let's hear two good ones before I send you off . . . Jasmine."

Holding up her book on babysitting, Jasmine said: "What are some ways to keep a baby sister busy?"

"Great question," I nodded. "Breshna?"

I gestured to Breshna who showed her book on New York City subways and said, "Who can ride the subway for free? Who can pay half fare?"

Edgar ended the share, "What is the Guggenheim? Where is it located?"

LINK

Remind students to do this work throughout the entire book and not just on one page. One way that writers elaborate is by asking "Who, What, Where, Why" questions.

"Writers, in just a moment you're going to go off and write. Remember, one way to get more information on each page is to answer 'Who, What, Where, Why' questions. When you go off to work today, make a goal to do this not only on *one* page, but on *every* page. You want to make your books fuller, answering all the different types of questions your readers might have on that particular page. Off you go!"

It may look like I'm doing a random call-and-response here and that miraculously, the kids I called on offered exemplar responses. (If only teaching were that convenient!) Actually, I called on students that I had listened in on, knowing that they could be relied on to share answers that would spur the understanding in the room.

Build Your Revision Repertoire

TODAY, you can demand volume, pushing all your students to revise in ways that help add more. For many, this will mean revisiting pages to elaborate. For some, this might even require a need to stick paper strips onto existing pages, or to add new pages to their books. Your writing center is probably already stocked with those revision materials (from the narrative unit) but if it isn't, do make sure you have extra paper, paper strips, tape, and staplers handy, and be ready to coach children to exercise independence at using these. In the mid-workshop, you distribute some of these tools to the students' tables.

As you will recall from the narrative unit, you can combine youngsters needing similar help into small groups. You might redo small groups from yesterday and reteach the minilesson in a small group, and you'll surely invent your own small groups to solve topics we don't anticipate. Remember that to gather the kids that have similar needs,

you just need to announce, "Anyone who is having trouble with . . . , I'm leading a group to help with that. Join us."

It will be easy to plan your own small groups because your role in these groups is minimal. Mostly, they provide a forum for kids to work together. After you tell the kids about a need you saw and offer a suggestion for moving forward, then you will channel the group to work in pairs to help each other. As they do that, you'll coach into one pair, then another, moving among them. Here are some strategies for small groups you are likely to conduct today.

SMALL GROUP

If some students are clumping unconnected information all on one page rather than writing across pages, pull them into a small group.

To prepare, print out "Breakfast." Have highlighters handy. Ask kids to bring their books. Set them up to work as partners.

"Writers, I've gathered you because writers of informational texts don't squish different information together. They look over their writing to ask: Could I organize this better? Might some of this belong on a different page?"

Then, hand each partnership a copy of "Breakfast." Prompt them to highlight only the sentences that have to do with "types of food." Suggest that the remaining information could go on its own separate page.

After students have done this, prompt students to open their book and do the same for their own writing, deciding where they might have mismatched information that could have its own different page. Have them explain their logic to their partner.

MID-WORKSHOP TEACHING   Writers Write Up a Storm

"Writers, I love seeing so many of you revising one page, then going to the next page to revise it. And the next! Will you count how many new lines you have added so far today?" I gave children time. "Look across your pages and add together the number of new lines you have added on every page.

"Don't tell me the number of new lines, but keep it in mind. You have fifteen more minutes to work, and by the end of today, you should *definitely* have added at least fifteen more lines of writing to your book. Some will do a *lot* more than that. Some of you may even add new pages! Get to work."

If some students are struggling with elaboration, pull them into a small group for shared writing.

"Writers, I gathered you here to solve a problem. The page about July 4th in our fireworks book is pretty short. Can you help me figure out what to add to it?" I displayed a page with the following words written across it: *The 4th of July is famous for fireworks.* "Let's read this page aloud together.

"Do you have any ideas how we could think of more to say?" I asked, setting the members of the small group up to recount the day's minilesson. "Oh, so you think we

could try rereading this and then asking one of those questions?" I asked. We reread the page—"The 4th of July is famous for fireworks," and then I murmured, "Why? Why the 4th of July?"

I said to the kids, "Turn and teach each other *why* fireworks and the 4th of July go together." I listened in, then jotted, "The 4th of the July is famous for fireworks. The day is the United States' birthday."

Then I said, "Keep going. Ask another question and answer it. I'll listen in."

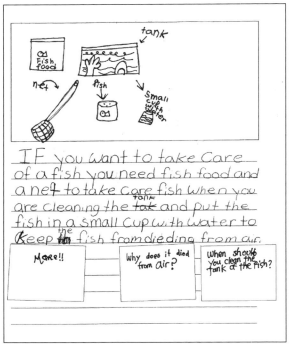

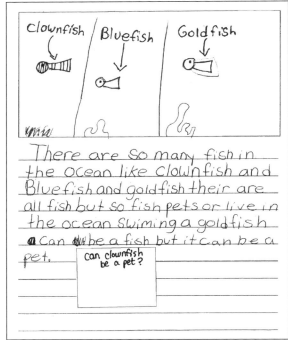

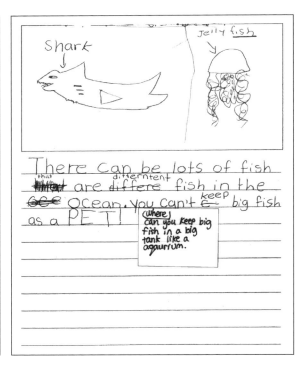

FIG. 2–2   Jahmiya's partner has helped her make plans for elaboration by placing "why," "when," and "where" questions across her book on pet fish.

Writing with Volume—and in Ways that Teach

Ask students to count how many lines they wrote, and congratulate their progress. Then set them up to read a page from their book that teaches a lot of information.

"Writers, time to stop. I know you want to keep going, but we have to do other things today. Before you stop, however, will you count how many lines of writing you did today?" I gave kids time to count. "How many of you wrote fifteen or more lines today?" Those kids raised their hands. "Stand and take a bow," I said. "That is nice work. And by tomorrow, we'll be aiming for even more writing.

"But here's the thing. It is also great if you wrote in a way that helped readers learn about your topic, so will you choose a page that you think *really* teaches a lot, and will you read that page to someone near you? See if the listener learns something about the topic. Go!"

WORKING WITH ENL STUDENTS

This session is already very supportive for ENLs:

◆ The session highlights turning to partners for support and feedback. Partnerships provide additional opportunities for kids to use the language of the writing process and genre. The share provides an opportunity for partners to reread their writing to each other.

◆ The work with "Who, What, Where, Why" questions provides students with examples, opportunities for repeated practice, options for ways to work, and clear steps.

◆ The conferring and small-group work includes a small group on shared writing. Shared writing provides additional experiences with listening, speaking, and rereading an information text.

To provide additional support for ENLs, you might:

◆ Create a mini-chart with "Who, What, Where, Why" for students to refer to as they revise their books, to support oral instruction.

Writing with Detail

Adding Exact Names, Numbers, Colors, Sizes, Shapes, Quotes

IN THIS SESSION

TODAY YOU'LL teach students that writers use *specifics* and not just generalizations. This means writing with exact names, numbers, colors, sizes, shapes, quotes.

TODAY STUDENTS will draft a second information book on a new topic. Channel students to write on paper with more lines. Expect to see more specific details in this second book. Students may also continue to revise their first information book.

GETTING READY

✔ Display the "How to Write an Information Book" anchor chart (see Connection, Teaching).

✔ Use a blank booklet to demonstrate adding details (see Teaching).

✔ Prepare to write in the air about a topic that needs elaborating. We chose Chinese food (see Teaching).

✔ Gather a few mentor texts that students can use as models when they revise (see Conferring and Small-Group Work).

✔ Make small copies of the "How to Write an Information Book" anchor chart for students to use as checklists (see Share).

✔ Today's minilesson video:

hein.pub/UTLINFO_3

Writing with Detail

Adding Exact Names, Numbers, Colors, Sizes, Shapes, Quotes

CONNECTION

Rally children to the important work of information writing by reminding them they are writing for their classroom library. Start kids thinking of another information book they will write today.

"You have an exciting job this month. You're not just writing these information books for yourselves, or for me. You're writing them for *this classroom library*." I pointed to the bins on the shelves. "This means taking your work as an information writer seriously.

Your intention is to recruit. Say this like writing for the library is an awesome priviledge.

"Today you're going to start a brand-new information book. But there's a big difference between the book you start today and the one that you've just finished." I leaned in to emphasize my next words. "The difference is that today's book will be a lot better written—because it's your second book. For one thing, your first draft will be *way* better because the strategies that you learned for revision are ones that you will now use to draft." As I spoke, I replaced the *Revise* sticky note on the anchor chart with a new one that said, *Draft and Revise*. "See what I just did? Growth means that yesterday's revisions will become today's first-draft strategies."

5. Draft
and Revise.

"To decide what this second book will be about, let's look back at the first sticky note on our chart." I pulled that Post-it from the chart and enlarged it.

1. Think of something you could teach.

I mulled over the suggestions. "What could I teach? What about something that I do? Well, I walk my dog. I work on my computer. I do laundry. I could certainly write an information book about any one of those things. What are some things *you* do, that you could teach others? Turn and talk." I allowed ten seconds for conversations to buzz before reconvening kids' attention.

I continued, "What about places I visit? Hmm, . . . I visit the mall. I visit the library. I visit the town where my grandparents live. You have different places you visit too. Close your eyes and recall those places, because any one of them could be your next book." After a few seconds, I said, "Turn and talk. Your next book could be about something you do, a place you visit, a topic you know about, a person you admire. You have twenty seconds to choose your topic." I looked at my timer, and said, "Go!"

"I have a tip for you that will always, forever, help you to be able to write more. It is a tip you have heard many times before, but here it is."

✦ Name the teaching point.

"Today I want to teach you one very important tip: write (and revise) with details. When writing information books, this means writing with *specifics* and not just with generalizations. It means writing with exact names, numbers, colors, sizes, shapes, quotes." I added a new bullet to our chart.

Teachers, topic selection can be super-quick. Resist the urge to spend endless time during your minilesson helping kids generate topics. That added time for topic selection often means that children second-guess their initial decision, trying to find the "best" topic. It is fine to go with a topic that is merely "good enough"; the best topic does not guarantee the best writing. When you maintain a fast pace in your minilesson and move on to the teaching point, you help kids decide and commit to a topic.

No matter how much time you devote to topic selection, there will always be some kids who tell you, "I can't decide what to write about." That's a small-group conversation, not a whole-class concern. Don't hold the rest of your writers hostage on the rug while a few uncertain kids are hemming and hawing.

TEACHING

Recruit students to think with you about a book you could write. Suggest you could fill it with generalizations, soliciting from them the suggestion that you need to write with specifics instead.

"Writers, let's pretend I am writing an information book about Chinese food." I grabbed a blank booklet from my writing folder and pointed to the first page. "In this book I will teach you all about Chinese food." Pointing to page 2, I dictated, "You eat food for the appetizer. Then you eat food for the main course. You also eat food for dessert." I turned the page and dictated, "You eat with special utensils."

Putting my imaginary book down, I feigned great pride and asked, "How do you like my information book? Did I do a great job?"

From around the room came cries of, "You didn't write with details." "You gotta say *what* the food is."

Nodding, I said, "You've nailed it. My book is not yet great, because I didn't include specific details—names, numbers, sizes, shapes, quotes. So what do I do?

"Think with me," I said, and recalled the first thing I'd written. "Hmm, . . . I wrote that at Chinese restaurants, people eat *food* for appetizers." I pointed to the bullet on my chart: names, numbers. "How about if I revise it so it sounds like this? I'm going to write-in-the-air for now and jot down some ideas later into our book."

> At Chinese restaurants, many people order *appetizers*. They often
> order *spring rolls* or *wonton soup*. Some people order one appetizer and
> some people order *two* or even *three* appetizers.

Debrief in ways that highlight the transferable work that you have done. Highlight the need to write with specific names, numbers, colors, shapes.

"Better, right? I did the work of teaching more information by adding more specific details. Did you notice how I added specific details, not just 'appetizers,' but the names of appetizers: spring rolls and wonton soup? Did you also notice how I also added more specific details by including the number of appetizers that people order?" The writers nodded.

ACTIVE ENGAGEMENT

Channel writers to practice improving other parts of the class book by turning generalizations into specifics. Remind them to write with specific names, colors, numbers, and shapes.

"Writers, keeping practicing this work. Talk about what the meals are like at Chinese restaurants, using specific details to teach as much as possible."

Teachers, the piece of writing referenced here returns in Session 5 when you help kids revise their introductions. You'll probably just want to write-in-the-air during this session, but there is a written version of this piece in the online resources.

If you want to point to names *on the bulleted chart as you say the names of the appetizers, and to* numbers *as you say the numbers, you make your point even more explicit. You could add colors if you want (although we weren't sure how to describe the colors of wonton soup).*

I listened as kids talked and then convened the class. "I heard so many specifics. I heard you suggest that the book say, 'Some people order moo shu pork, which includes six flat circular pancakes and some shredded pork.' Some suggested that the book could say many meals have broccoli. I even heard you say the broccoli looks like little green trees. Tony suggested that instead of saying 'People eat with utensils,' it would be good to say, 'People usually eat with chopsticks made of plastic or wood. Sometimes they come in long, paper envelopes that have paintings of bamboo trees.'

"Writers, in the book you write today (and in all the information writing you do from this day forward), always remember to write with interesting details. Remember that Tony didn't say, 'People at Chinese restaurants eat with utensils' but instead, 'People at Chinese restaurants often eat with chopsticks. Sometimes these come in long, paper envelopes.' I can just picture those envelopes that hold the chopsticks, can't you?"

Debrief what you just did so writers to make it feel replicable.

I summed up, "When you are writing or revising, remember that nonfiction books are written with specific, detailed information. Instead of 'people eat food,' you could say 'people eat moo shu pork.' Instead of saying 'the meal has broccoli in it,' you could say, 'the meal has little stalks of broccoli that look like tiny trees.'"

LINK

Remind writers of all of the strategies they know to teach readers.

"As you go off to write today, remember that your job as writers of information books is to teach readers as much as you can about your topic. And, your job is to use all that you've learned to write a second book that is *way* better than your first. To teach well and to write well, you need to include a lot of interesting specifics about your topic."

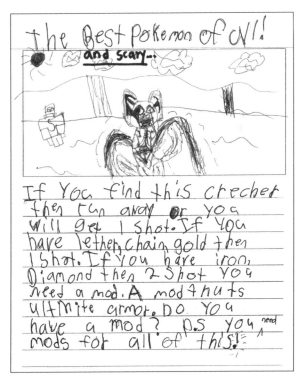

FIG. 3–1 This expert's writing crackles with specific details because the topic is close to his heart.

Predictable, Quick Interventions to Keep the Whole Class Writing Up a Storm!

Offer compliments in ways that build your students' identities as information writers.

- "You're not just teaching with words. I see you're also labeling your pictures like a teacher. You are so much like _____ (*mentor author*)! I'm leaving one of his books beside you so you can notice how he writes longer captions for his diagrams. Maybe you'll decide to do some of that too!"

- "I notice that you're using big vocabulary words related to your topic—your writing is full of authority because of that. Keep using all the words that go with your topic. You're not only teaching the reader about the topic, you are also helping the reader talk like he's an expert on it."

- "Wow, you've added a sidebar to this page. Who taught you to do that? Your book did? That is *amazing*. And these words you've bolded. You are such a reader of information texts. Are there other spots in your writing where you're planning to do this?"

MID-WORKSHOP TEACHING
Writers Comb Their New Lessons into Old Texts

"Writers, I just saw something *so* cool. Some of you are going back to your first nonfiction book and you are taking it out of the red-dot side of your folder—out of the 'I'm done' side of your folder—and you are revising it! You already asked 'Who, What, Where, Why' questions, and this time I saw you adding specific names, colors, quotes, shapes . . . the works!

"You are truly being like professional writers when you take new insights and comb those through texts you thought were done. Writers have a saying, 'When you are done, you have just begun.' That saying describes your work. I am proud as punch of you!"

SMALL GROUP

Provide additional support to writers who are writing with generalizations.

You might notice that despite your best teaching in the minilesson, some writers are writing with generalizations and exaggerations. Gather these writers together and say, "Writers, there are a few words that signal that you are not writing with enough detail. These are words like *a lot*, *lots*, and *stuff*. Take a moment and scan your draft for these words." Next, move from writer to writer coaching them to write with specific details and concrete information: numbers, names, quotes, descriptions, facts. For example, a child who writes, "Dogs eat a *lot*, I mean a *lot*. They love, love, love to eat. Sometimes they try to eat your head off," can be channeled to write specifically about dog biscuits, meat, bones . . .

Use Checklists as Powerful Reminders

Talk up the importance of using reminders in life, and share that writers use checklists to help them remember important work they need to do.

"Writers, have you ever heard of people who tie string around their fingers to remind themselves to do something? It is true—some people do that. Some people wear little machines that remind them to do things—like I know some people who wear Fitbits that tell them how many steps they have taken in a day. Those people look at their Fitbits and think, 'Oh no, I *forgot* to walk today!' That sounds funny, but it is true.

"Writers don't wear Fitbits, but they have their own ways to remind themselves about what they have done, and what they still need to do. One thing they do is to make checklists. Do you remember how we made small copies of a chart from the narrative unit and used them as checklists? That worked so well for us that I thought we should do that again."

Invite partners to work together, checking to see if they have included the important elements of good information writing in their own writing. Hand out checklists for this work.

"If you want, with your partner, you can look over everything we have learned about good information writing, and see if you did those things in both of your books. You game?"

The kids were eager, so I distributed small copies of the "How to Write an Information Book" chart to use as checklists and students set to work. As they worked, I called out in a voiceover, "If you haven't yet done something, help each other. That's what partners are for. You can make some super-quick revisions right now."

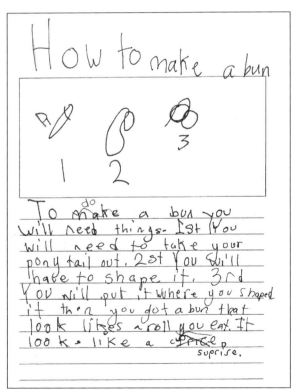

FIG. 3–2 Jahmiya uses sentence starters to help with structure: FIrst you will . . . Second you will . . .

WORKING WITH ENL STUDENTS

This session is already very supportive for ENLs:

◆ You model how to make plans for revision and refer to a step-by-step class chart. This reinforces academic language usage and encourages students to apply this language to their own planning.

◆ In the share, you convert the now-familiar anchor chart into a checklist, allowing students to use familiar language as a support for self- and peer assessment.

To provide additional support for ENLs, you might:

◆ Offer students more opportunity for oral rehearsal. Prior to writing, pull a small group around thinking and planning for a new information book.

◆ Annotate a published information book marking places where the author wrote with exact details to provide additional examples. Extend this work by also noting predictable sentence frames.

Reading Your Writing through the Eyes of a Stranger

Revision

IN THIS SESSION

TODAY YOU'LL teach students that writers reread their writing with the eyes of a stranger, and they use what they see to improve what's on their pages.

TODAY STUDENTS will revise their second and first information books. Some students may need to finish drafting their second book before revising both books.

GETTING READY

✔ Make sure that students have access to revision supplies, including revision strips, flaps, Post-its, glue, and scissors.

✔ Ask students to bring their writing folders and pencil or pen to the meeting area (see Teaching).

✔ Display the revisions to the Bill of Rights using a document camera (or an enlarged copy). A full copy of the document is available in the online resources (see Teaching).

✔ Display the "Revision Symbols" chart (see Teaching).

✔ Print copies of Sentence Starter cards to distribute to students (see Conferring and Small-Group Work).

✔ Today's minilesson video:

hein.pub/UTLINFO_4

Reading Your Writing through the Eyes of a Stranger
Revision

CONNECTION

Tell about how a stranger visiting your classroom helped you see the room with new eyes. Suggest the parallels to writing, pointing out that writers need to develop stranger's eyes.

"I want to tell you something that happened yesterday in this classroom. While you were out at gym class, Ms. Torres, our principal, walked in with a man I'd never seen before. He was dressed in a suit, so he looked like a stranger to our school. The stranger stood in the doorway, looked around our classroom, wrote something on a notepad and left. But here is the important thing. When that stranger stood there in the doorway and looked around our classroom—like this," and I enacted him looking around closely, "*I* looked around our room too.

"That might seem like nothing. I mean, you are probably thinking, 'Yeah, so what? Don't you look around our room all the time?' But the important thing is this: when I looked around our room through the eyes of that stranger, I saw things I'd never seen before. I saw things that had been here all along that I had stopped noticing. Like, I noticed that the papers on that bulletin board need more tacks.

"Try it. Stand up and pretend you're the stranger seeing this classroom for the very first time. See the room as that stranger might have seen it." I gave kids a minute to look without talking, then said, "Tell the person nearest to you what you notice."

I listened as kids talked, and then nodding, convened the class. "I'm the same as you. I noticed some beauty that I don't usually see, like the way the sun shines onto the plants in that window. But I also noticed some less-than-beautiful things, like the plants look thirsty. And those stack of papers in the corner. I bet it has been there for weeks without me even seeing it!"

Make the connection to writing. Writing, too, needs to be viewed through the eyes of a stranger.

"Here is my point. It's good to see your own classroom with new eyes. And it's also good to see your own *writing* with new eyes. Now, I could say to you, 'Let's line up and walk down the hallway to another classroom. Let's find a stranger to read your writing. Or let's go out onto the street and recruit passersby to read our writing.'"

Writers do not need to learn to do an infinite number of things—but they need to learn to actually do those things, and that's not easy. As a teacher of writing, you need to find new ways to recruit your students to do the work that is most essential. Certainly one big thing that a writer needs to do is to shift from being the writer to being a reader. Writers need to get distance from their own drafts and to use that distance to nudge revisions. Revision, after all, means just that: re-vision. This session aims to teach children to "look again" at their writing.

❖ Name the teaching point.

"Today I want to teach you that writers need to learn how to become a stranger to their own writing. And after rereading your writing with the eyes of a stranger, you need to be able to use what you see with those stranger's eyes to improve what's on your page."

TEACHING

Channel students to see their own writing through the eyes of a stranger, making marginal notes to indicate places where they noticed something. Suggest these are places that merit revision.

"Try it. Take out the book you wrote yesterday, your second information book. Open to the first page. Put on imaginary glasses that make you a stranger. See if you notice things that you overlooked before. You will find some things that are fabulous, some things that seem a little confusing, and some things that are not perfect and need fixing up. When you see something, put a little dot in the margin next to what you see. This will be quick, so in half a minute, you'll have a bunch of little dots on this first page.

"Writers, you're going to have time today to reread the books that you have written so far with a stranger's eyes, noticing things that work and things also that don't quite work. The things you notice will form a 'to-do' list for you, because the parts of your writing that you love can be expanded upon, and the mess-ups can be fixed. You'll end up going from rereading to revising."

Caution that revisions can't just be added at the end, but need to be placed appropriately. Suggest writers use tools to do that work and show revisions of the Bill of Rights to make your point.

"But writers—before you head off to continue rereading, can I give you another tip? In your first book, you revised by asking a 'Who, What, Where, Why' question or two, and adding on. I know you probably plan to do more of that today, but here's a tip. It won't always work just to add the new stuff onto the end of your pages. For example, if one page is about what dogs eat, and you first tell about their breakfast, then their supper, and then you want to revise by telling more about the food they eat for their breakfast, you can't just stick the *breakfast* part at the *end* of the page! That page would look sort of crazy-pants: dog's breakfast, dog's supper, dog's breakfast again. Do you see that's a problem?

"So what to do?

"For an answer, I would to turn your attention to one of the most powerful texts ever written in human history," I lowered my voice for the dramatic announcement. "The Bill of Rights! It is part of the Constitution of the United States, which has endured for more than two centuries. The Founders of this nation—the most responsible writers ever—used revision symbols." I placed the image under the document camera.

You are describing this as if the kids will see tons of things. They may not, but you always want to convey high expectations, because your expectations become the ceiling for your kids. Speak with utter confidence about how much they will notice, and if a child doesn't see much, act surprised. Then join that child in reading her writing and vow to find beauty in the first two lines. Look hard: you can see it!

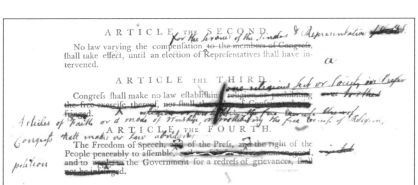

Archival Research Catalog www.archives.gov

In an awed voice, I added, "These are real revisions. *Historic* revisions. Turn and tell the person beside you what the Founders did with their black pens to revise that printed draft of this part of the Constitution."

I allowed about fifteen seconds for children to talk before recalling their attention. "Thumbs up if you noticed these little symbols they used to insert new words right into the middle of the page." I pointed out the carets. "Thumbs up if you noticed that they crossed out words that didn't work. Nod if you noticed that they added new words—and again, added them into the middle and sides of the page.

"The people who made this country looked at the first draft of the Constitution through the eyes of strangers, and they saw things that were confusing, that needed to be fixed. And they revised their first draft to make it the best it could be. They did this by inserting new words right into the middle of the text, crossing out other words. And they didn't just do that *once*. They kept adding and fixing and changing words around, trying to get them to be better.

"Like other writers, they used symbols to help them make their revisions simply and clearly. Here's a chart with some symbols that you can use, too."

Revision Symbols

Symbols	Job	Example
(Box + arrow)	Shift this text here	Sparklers are the simplest kind of fireworks. They are just a stick with a sparkle on the end. You hold them. [box:] The stick has come chemicals on the end that makes them sparkle.
(Curly)	Delete this word/part	Rockets are the ~~fanciest~~ fancier. There are rocket fireworks that shoot straight up only in a spiral. They go up and then down, like rockets, only then they die.
(Caret)	Insert word or phrase	The best fireworks make giant ∧colorful flowers in the sky. They can be pink or blue or white

ACTIVE ENGAGEMENT

Channel kids to talk about the revisions they imagine they could make on their books.

"Right now, will you tell your partner three things you can imagine doing to make your book better?" The partners talked, and I listened in. "Show your partner where on your page you might revise—and tell your partner whether you plan to use arrows or flaps . . . or what?"

After a bit I convened the class and said, "Powerful stuff! I heard several of you say that you cannot wait to try out these new tools." I pointed to the list of revision symbols.

"Writers, I watched Brendan as he reread this page in his venom book," I said as I projected Brendan's book.

The Eastern Brown Snake is the most venomous snake in the world.

It lives in Australia.

It pounces on or bites a threat.

It lives in the ground or in a cave.

"Brendan said that he's going to box out and move this line," I said pointing to the last sentence, "to right after this sentence about the snake living in Australia because both those sentences are about where the snake lives." I leaned into the class and continued, "But the best part was that Brendan wasn't finished with his revisions! He also made plans to add a flap here," I said, pointing to the third sentence, "to teach about what kinds of things are a threat to the Eastern Brown Snake."

LINK

Channel the kids to look over their writing with the eyes of a stranger, imagining revisions, and to use asterisks and arrows to insert revisions into the middle of their drafts.

"Today I want to remind you that distance helps a writer. The best writers look over whatever they've written with the distant eyes of a stranger to ask, 'What works? What needs *more* work? What puts me to sleep? What should be changed?'"

I held up scissors and giant Post-its. "The best writers use tools to make sure that when they add information, they add it into the right places on their pages. Get working. Once you finish revising this second book, I know you are going to want to go back and also revise your first book. Some of you may have time to start a new book as well."

FIG. 4–1 Raby's self-edits reflect a new investment in his own writing.

Support Students in Making Revisions that Are Meaningful

Coach Writers to Revise Pages They Think They've Finished

- **To a student who seems resistant to revision:** "I hear you say that you like your book just the way it is, that it requires no revision. Would you rather write a new book than work on improving the one you already started?" Sometimes the resistance to revision will melt away when a youngster realizes the option is the empty page.

- **To a student who is revising in minor ways:** "You just made that sentence better with a tiny caret. That's a good thing to do. But pro writers don't just revise by adding a word, a phrase . . . they also add major big chunks. Like pro writers sometimes think—'Right here, I could say half a page more.' To do that, they usually cut apart the page, tape in a whole half-page, then fill it up! If I helped you do that, would you be willing? We could then show all the kids. You could be their professor. Professor of Revision."

- **To a student who worries about "messing up" the appearance of her page with revision marks:** "If you look at the manuscripts of *Harry Potter* or *Charlie and the Chocolate Factory*, guess what you'll find? Not neat, perfect little sentences, no way! You'll see arrows and carets and crossed-out stuff and scribbles in the margins. That's how Dahl and Rowling wrote. Make your draft beautiful with some real revisions, some real writing."

- **Make a major public case out of instances when kids do revise.** *[Pause the room.]* "Wow! Some of you are doing such professional work! I just saw one writer use an arrow to add a detail into her draft. So cool! There is also a writer in this room who has the courage to rewrite the lead to her chapter. I am so proud!"

- "What you wrote here is fascinating! I had no idea! You are being my teacher. Listen, could you explain more about that . . . ?" Listen to a bit. "Oh my gosh, you *have* to put that on the page. Wait, wait, here, I've got paper for you. Write that down, just the way you said it to me." Dictate the start of it back to the student as he scribes. "After you write that, I'll show you how to stick it into your book."

MID-WORKSHOP TEACHING **Celebrate Revisions that Involve Subtracting and Dividing as Well as Adding**

"Writers, I am so pleased to see that you are not just adding information, you are also subtracting and dividing. Think for a minute: Why would writers *subtract* information?" I paused for a moment. "Ideas?"

Kids pitched thoughts: perhaps the information didn't go in that book or on that page. Perhaps they had repeated themselves. Perhaps it was boring. I raised the ante.

"And why might an author get involved in division?" I asked. "Talk to each other because it is a challenging question." After a bit, I said, "Writers, I agree. Sometimes you start a page and think everything you are writing goes together and goes on that page. After a while you think, 'Wait. I have stuff about two different things stuck together on this one page.' So then it becomes important to divide the page up—and the tool for doing that is . . . scissors!

"As you get back to work, please time yourself so that you get time to reread your first book as well as your second with a stranger's eyes. You have a lot to do!"

Use sentence starters as a tool to help struggling writers add more to each page.

- To get ready, print Sentence Starter cards for each child. Bring a bin of revision supplies (colored pens, Post-its, flaps, and glue) to the rug.

- Gather kids close. Say: "I called you over so that we can revise together. Right now, find a page of your writing that looks a little empty and place a Post-it there."

- Explain that information writers don't just put their first thought on a page and stop. They revise by adding more.

- Hand children the Sentence Starter cards and set them to work in pairs to orally rehearse the lines that they may add.

- Channel partners to help each other in using arrows, Post-its, and flaps to add these lines onto their chosen pages. Allow kids to use excessive Post-its. The tools will lure them on!

- As kids work, coach:
  "Reread. Make sure it makes sense."
  "Your piece is becoming longer! Yes!"
  "It would be so cool if you reread this one more time and saw even *more* things you could add."

Sentence Starters

- For example . . .
- This means . . .
- Have you ever wondered . . .
- Some people don't realize . . .

Glory in Messy Rough Drafts

Rally your students to choose their best revision to display for a gallery walk. Channel kids to admire the masterpieces and to note possible topics for tomorrow's writing.

"Writers, your revisions are beautiful. Would you find a page where you did a lot of revision and open your book to that page? Clean up your work area so the only thing on display is your one, well-loved page."

After the kids did that, I said, "I think you can guess what I suggest we do to end today. Let's think of this classroom as a gallery, as a museum, and take some time to gape at the masterpieces on display. Notice the revisions that your classmates have made, the ways they took a so-so page and made it better.

"As you admire each other's writing, will you think about what your next book might be about? Most of you have finished writing a second book and will be ready tomorrow to start a third book. Pay attention to possible topics.

"No talking, just admiring."

WORKING WITH ENL STUDENTS

This session is already very supportive for ENLs:

◆ Partnerships support language development and are especially helpful when a writer rereads his or her writing to revise it. For example, writers often have a hard time detecting confusion in their own texts, but partners can see and point out confusing parts and help support revisions.

◆ Conferring and Small-Group Work provides elaboration sentence starters that scaffold writers.

To provide additional support for ENLs, you might:

◆ Provide students with a mentor information text that you have marked up and labeled to illustrate different ways writers can revise their writing. This could be a published text or your own demonstration writing.

◆ For additional practice, invite a group of writers to read and revise a piece of writing together.

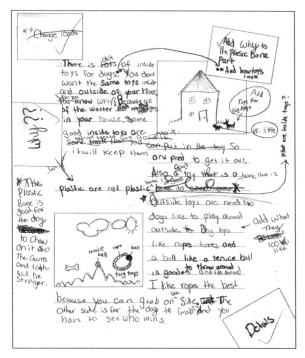

FIG. 4–2   We love it when bulletin boards feature work like this!

First Things First

Beginnings Matter

IN THIS SESSION

TODAY YOU'LL teach students that information writers make their introductions special.

TODAY STUDENTS will draft a third information book. Expect to see them trying to make a special beginning and ending. Students may also revise the beginnings and endings of their earlier books.

GETTING READY

✔ Distribute a nonfiction book from the class library to each partnership (see Teaching).

✔ Prepare to write a list of ways to make a beginning special on chart paper (see Teaching).

✔ Display the list of topics you shared with a small group in Session 1 (see Active Engagement). 👏

✔ Prepare to add another bullet to the "How to Write an Information Book" anchor chart (see Mid-Workshop Teaching). 👏

✔ Today's minilesson video:

hein.pub/UTLINFO_5

First Things First
Beginnings Matter

CONNECTION

Ask kids to bring their first and second books to the meeting area, then lay them side by side to study signs of progress.

"Writers, most of you have two or even three information books that you've created so far. Could you bring your writing folders *and* a brand-new blank booklet with you to the rug right now?" I waited for students to assemble.

"Now, put your first and second books in front of you, side by side—the first book on the left, then the most recent book on the right. Here is a huge, important question. How is the most recent book better than the first one? Before you answer, think why this is such a huge, important question."

I paused. Nodding as if I'd heard their response and agreed 100 percent, I said, "Yes! Absolutely. The differences between these two books show how much you have grown—and I've seen you guys grow in leaps and bounds."

"Right now, study the ways that your second book is better." I gave them a little time to get started and then voiced over, "How many of you have more lines of writing, or more pages of writing, in your most recent book?" Many youngsters signaled yes, or maybe, and I embraced their signals. "Fabulous! Give yourselves a pat on the back."

After a few moments, I interrupted. "Writers, do any of you have more specifics in the second book—names, numbers, colors, shapes? You do? Great!

"Writers, hold up the blank booklet you brought." As kids held up their books, I leaned in. "The book you are holding is going to be your very best one yet. It will be the best because you are going to do *all of the things* you have learned so far—and more."

❖ **Name the teaching point.**

"Today I want to teach you one more thing that information writers do. Information writers try to make their introductions special. That's it. They know their beginnings matter and they try to make them special."

Research is clear that people don't get better very quickly just be doing something again and again. They get better by deliberate, goal-driven practice. You are rallying your students to set goals for themselves.

TEACHING

Recruit kids to help you consider ways to make the lead of the book you just wrote more special. Ask them to help you scan leads in nonfiction books you have on hand to generate ideas.

"Do you remember our book about Chinese meals? We said it would start, 'In this book I will teach you all about Chinese food.'"

I paused as if to think. "What do you think? Is it special?" The class shook their heads and I agreed.

"So how do we add pizzazz to the introduction of that book? Hmm, . . . What do you think?"

The kids looked at each other, at me, and shrugged. I asked, "What if we pull some nonfiction books off our shelves, and I give you and your partner each a book, and you check it out? See if the authors give you some ideas for how to write a special beginning. They won't all have a special introduction, but if yours does, work with your partner to try to figure out what the author did that we could try, too."

I distributed books, and circulated, hearing lines read aloud.

If you can quickly tap the class for suggestions, do so. Otherwise just report that you heard kids talking about a few ways to make leads special. Use the class book to illustrate each way.

"Call out some ideas," I said. From students' shoutouts, I gleaned some suggestions:

> To make your beginning special
> - Paint a picture with words
> - Ask readers a question
> - Tell a little story or an interesting fact

"Let's try those methods and come up with ways to start our book about Chinese restaurants," I said. "Let's think of a word-picture you could paint. Hmm, . . . imagine you are walking into a Chinese restaurant. What do you see? Hmm, . . . You picturing it? How about this?" I said, dictating a possible beginning:

> The restaurant is filled with little red and white booths and every table has a small bamboo plant in the middle of it.

The project you ask kids to participate in here—looking at how authors start their nonfiction books—could take a day or a week, but today you're asking kids to do this in just a minute or two. Your goal isn't to do this particularly well, but rather to show kids that the list of ways to make a lead special doesn't emerge from thin air—it comes from looking at what other authors have done and trying to put what you see into words. The books you select can be any books, and they won't all match the list you share later in this minilesson.

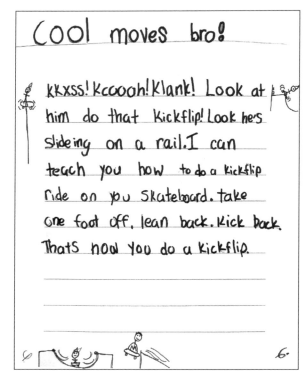

FIG. 5–1 Nicholas' mentor author uses sound effects.

"That would be a great beginning for our book, wouldn't it? Let's try another way to make a special beginning. How about—we could ask a question related to Chinese restaurants. Like . . .

> Does your family sometimes go out to dinner at a
> Chinese restaurant?

"Or we could tell a very teeny story related to Chinese restaurants":

> One time my family went to a Chinese restaurant that had a grill as
> the table. "Sit around the table," they told us. A cook came out and
> started twirling an egg on the tip of a spatula. Soon he was juggling
> with two eggs! That was a fun surprise!

Debrief in a way that highlights the replicable work that you have done.

"Writers, we just tried three different ways to make the start to our Chinese restaurant book special. We could have tried other ways to make it special—these aren't the only ways. The important thing is that whenever any of us write an information book, we should try to make the beginning special. We'll later go back to our fireworks book and revise that beginning too."

ACTIVE ENGAGEMENT

Channel writers to first home in on a topic they'll write about today and to then use the minilesson to help them generate a special way to start their book.

"Writers, you will be writing another book today—so take a sec now to think of what you'll write about. You looked at each other's books during our share yesterday and got some great ideas. You can also look back at our list of topics. Tell each other what you are thinking your topic will be today. Go!"

I displayed the "Topic for Information Writing" list of prompts for generating topics that I'd shared in a small group earlier in the unit.

After a minute, I said, "Thumbs up if you have an idea." Most children signaled. "Before you think about how you might make a special beginning, think about what you might write about on each page. Take out your blank book and touch page 1, page 2, telling your partner what you might write about on those pages."

The kids did that and then I voiced over. "All of you, turn back to page 1 now. Touch page 1." I waited. "In your mind, write-in-the-air how you might start this page with a question." I left a bit of silence. "Now try a harder way to start your book—with a word picture. Imagine walking up to or into your topic. Say, 'I walked into/up to . . . I saw . . .' What do you see?"

LINK

Don't break the spell. Channel kids to record what they were just thinking, while sitting in the meeting area. Once you see a youngster has a strong start on his or her book, send that child off.

Whispering, trying not to break the spell, I said, "Get one of those special beginnings down, fast. It's too good to forget." As kids wrote, I moved among them, gesturing for them to carry their books back to their work spots and to continue working.

After the kids who were off to a good start had been sent off, I gathered the remaining youngsters into a small group to help them settle on a topic. To do that, I gave them less choice. "Tell me what you do a lot when you are home?" I asked. When they answered (watch TV, hang out, help my mom clean), I channeled them to write books on those topics. "Try starting with a question." I suggested a few question stems. "'Do you . . . I do!' 'Have you ever . . .' 'Do you know a lot about . . . I do!'"

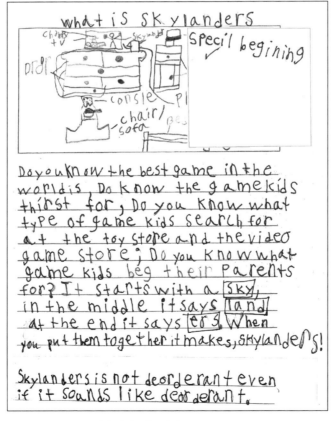

FIG. 5–2   Lucas added this lead during revision.

Support Students to Draw on All They Know

Y OUR MINILESSON will have helped your class get started writing today, so most of your conferring and small-group work will be aimed at reminding them to use all they know to make the rest of their draft the best it can be.

Remind Students To Use All They Know To Make Their Draft the Best It Can Be	
If . . .	**Then . . .**
A writer shows little or no growth between the first two books written earlier in the bend and the one he is currently writing.	Hold the reader accountable by placing those first two books alongside this new one. "Your goal is not just to make the start of this book better than the other two books you have written. It is to make every *page* better. Look back at a page you wrote in your last book. Leave that page out so you can see it. As you work, make sure this new page is *way* better than that page from your last book. What are some ways you can make it better?" Help this writer list some goals.
A writer seems to have exhausted his or her energy for writing.	Build conversation around this topic. Ask probing questions and be a rapt audience to get this writer to talk. Channel this writer to put thoughts down.
A writer has detailed sketches but not enough writing.	Invite this writer to teach you about this sketch. Ask questions to help her say more. "What is *this* part of the sketch showing? If you had to zoom in to one part of this sketch to teach more, which part would you pick? Why?" And finally, "You've taught me a ton. I heard you describe . . ." List some categories of information this writer just mentioned. Then say, "The words you said created powerful teaching. Put these words down."

"Writers, can I have your attention for a minute? I recently heard a very interesting saying—I need your help to figure out what it means. 'Good-byes are as important as hellos.' What do you think that means?"

I allowed about thirty seconds for children to talk before I called for their attention. "I think you're right. I think what you said might be true of writing too." I held up an information book, displaying its cover and then flipping the book open, "The beginning of each page greets the reader with a special beginning, but . . ." I flipped to the last page. "No information book screeches to an abrupt halt. Writers work to make their endings special, too. They make up the last lines your reader will read. They are your last chance to give your reader something to remember about your topic.

"I want to teach you that information writers not only create special beginnings, they also create special endings by reteaching the big parts of the topic in a few short sentences and by adding a new thought."

I added a bullet to the anchor chart.

"Right now, look at the words you've ended your book with. Ask yourself: What are the big things about your topic that the reader shouldn't forget? Mention them quickly to remind the reader—and then add a final thought about your topic."

Symphony Share

Conduct a symphony share. Invite kids to choose a favorite special part they wrote in their books to first share with a partner, and then share with the class.

"Writers, it's time to gather for a symphony share. You remember how these go. I'll act as conductor and when I point at you, you'll sing out something special you wrote today. It could be a line or two of your introduction or another special part in your book.

"Quickly, look across your writing. Once you've found a part you are particularly proud of, get ready to share it with a partner first. Take turns rehearsing the part you select. Then we'll have our symphony. Go!" As kids rehearsed, I called out, "Don't just *read* your special part—give it the pizzazz it deserves! Use some expression!

After a minute, I gathered them back. "Ready?" As I pointed at kids, they shared the special parts of their writing, reading aloud with flair. "Bravo! Your information writing is spectacular!"

WORKING WITH ENL STUDENTS

This session is already very supportive for ENLs:

◆ Seeing evidence of growth is important for ENLs. Today's connection allows them to see improvement from their first books to their second.

◆ Students are familiar with the class book (Session 1), allowing them to focus on the new work.

To provide additional support for ENLs, you might:

◆ Allot more time for students to orally rehearse their special beginning before they write.

◆ Add sentence starters to the "To Make Your Beginning Special" chart, like "Do you . . . ?" and "Have you ever . . . ?"

◆ Annotate published information books with students, popping out ways the author made her beginning special.

"How Do I Write This Kind of Writing Well?"

IN THIS SESSION

TODAY YOU'LL teach students that when writers write or revise, they draw on all they know about good information writing.

TODAY STUDENTS will revise *all* of the information books they have written so far. Some students might draft a fourth information book.

GETTING READY

✔ Before the session, put special "Revision" Post-its in each child's folder.

✔ Print out copies of "Libraries" to distribute to students (see Teaching). 👏

✔ Prepare to construct a chart titled "What Makes for Great Information Writing?" (see Teaching). 👏

✔ Display three bare-bones pages of a child's piece titled "Legos" that you and the class will extend (see Active Engagement). 👏

✔ Prepare to show a short excerpt of a video of a TED Talk by Thomas Suarez, a twelve-year-old app developer. Be prepared to play the video from 1:35 to 2:30. A link to the video is in the online resources (see Share). 👏

✔ Today's minilesson video:

hein.pub/UTLINFO_6

46

"How Do I Write This Kind of Writing Well?"

CONNECTION

Ask students to bring their folder to the meeting space and announce that today they have a choice: write one final book or revise and finish ongoing ones.

"Writers, you all have three, maybe four, information books in your folder." Once the class was settled, I continued. "We have just two more days before we celebrate the great information writing that you have done and put your books in our class library. Today you have a choice: You can write another cool book *or* you can finish and revise the two or three books you've already written so far.

"Whatever you decide, it will help to be clear in your mind about what makes an information book great. Yesterday you talked about how to make beginnings special. Today your question is bigger: What makes information writing good? What do information writers aim to do?"

Use an analogy to rally your students to value the instruction you'll be giving them today.

"Have any of you ever played darts? Right now, imagine we have a dart board here, and you are holding a dart in your hand. If you want the dart to do the right thing, what do you need to do?"

The kids called out that they'd need to aim it well. I nodded. "Right now, pretend to throw that imaginary dart and watch what you do." I gestured to suggest the dart board was on the easel beside me, and stepped out of the way of the flying darts. "What I saw is that you fixed your eyes on the bull's-eye. You stared right at the red circle in the middle and then you aimed your arm right toward that goal, am I right?"

The kids agreed. "So what does that have to do with the work you are going to do today? Remember, you can write one last book, or you can look back on all the books you have written so far, and either way, you need to . . . what? (No, not throw darts!)"

In your own life, think about how empowering it is when someone gives you choices. Giving kids choices is a way to tap their energy.

SESSION 6: "HOW DO I WRITE THIS KIND OF WRITING WELL?"

Name the teaching point.

"Writers, today I want to teach you that as writers write and revise information books, they keep in mind what they are aiming to do. As you write or revise your own information books, it's important to keep your target in mind and to draw on all you know about good information writing to write as well as you can."

TEACHING

Channel students to study a fairly simple text that embodies the qualities of effective information writing.

"I thought it might help you to look over a little piece of information writing I've written. I've tried to make this be a bull's-eye text for you. I think this little piece of writing shows most of the qualities of good information writing that you should be aiming for right now."

I distributed copies. "As we read, let's remember to think, 'What makes for great information writing?' You might mark or jot anything you notice this author did to make this text effective."

> ### Libraries
>
> Most towns have schools, police stations, a flag pole . . . and of course, a library. Some libraries are giant and some are small, but whether they are big or small, most libraries are similar to each other. Do you want to know ways that they are similar? Then keep reading!
>
> The first thing you see when you go in a library is the checkout desk, and a librarian who works there. Usually librarians are ready to help you. You just have to ask. In some libraries you return books by giving the stack to the librarian, and in other libraries there are machines that scan the books. When you go to check out books, too, some libraries have scanners and some use cards in the back of the book, pens, stamp pads, and lists. Either way, the librarian keeps track of who is taking a book out of a library and who is bringing the book back.
>
> Usually libraries put all the biographies together and all the fiction books together and so on. There is a numbering system called the Dewey Decimal System that many libraries follow. If you see the chart, it will tell you the numbers where you can find different kinds of books. Some of them are alphabetically ordered and some of them are not.
>
> Libraries have systems to check out books and to return them, but that's not the important thing. The important thing is that communities have a place to go to borrow books, to find books, and to read books free of charge.

WHAT MAKES FOR GREAT...
information writing?
↳ It has a beginning.
  The writer seemed to try to make the beginning special.

↳ It teaches readers a lot about the topic.
↳ It teaches details like facts, numbers, quotes and tips.
↳ It has an ending.

"So, what did I do as an information writer that you could aim to do in your writing? What makes for effective information writing? When you have one idea, put a thumb up." I paused until most students had a thumb raised. "Turn and share what you've noticed."

Reconvene writers and ask some to share their ideas about what makes for effective information writing. After listening for a bit, write the list below as if this is what your students have said.

"Amir, what did you and your partner name?"

"It's about libraries?" Amir said. I nodded and tried to rework Amir's thinking, so it would pertain to information writing more generally, "And there is *lots* of information about that one topic, isn't there?" I said as I jotted that on chart paper. I left space to record a later comment about the beginning, so that the completed list would roughly follow a beginning-middle-end structure.

As we continued, one student named "There is a special beginning." Soon we had constructed a chart.

As students talk, listen to those who essentially say what you want them to say—see the "What Makes for Great Information Writing?" chart. You may even rephrase what they say. "So are you saying the good information writing contains lots of information on a topic? When I call on you, will you say that?" Listen also to assess what your students have learned thus far.

Teachers, you'll see that the "What Makes for Great Information Writing?" chart only contains things you have taught in the unit. You could add other features of good information writing—that it is structured by subtopics, includes transitions, and so forth—but you could also let those float away for now, planning to add them later after the whole class has had more time to talk about those. In general, lists such as this are most effective if they round up learning the students have already done rather than functioning as a crash course that aims to teach ten things all at once.

ACTIVE ENGAGEMENT

Involve writers in quickly studying another information piece and naming ways the writer can revise.

"Writers, you've come up with a great list. That should help you aim well when you write. Do you think you're game to use the list to help me? Remember my neighbor, Otis? He asked me for help with his information writing. He wants to make it even better! Do you think you and your partner could look with me at Otis's information writing and see if you have some ideas for ways he could make his writing even better? That might help you look at your own writing, later, and get ideas for making it even better too."

This imaginary kid, Otis, shows up across this series. Otis gives you a way to engage the class in working with a shared text that has all the problems their writing is apt to have.

This book will teach about Legos.

Legos are a toy that people build with.
You can build lots of things with them.

Kids and adults can both build with Legos.
Babies shouldn't play with Legos.

"What do you think? What works? What could make this writing even better? Tell your partner and use the chart to be specific." Students began talking and I coached, referring them back to the chart often.

"Writers, I heard many of you say that Otis wrote information about one topic, Legos. He has information on that topic, but he doesn't have *lots* of information and he could give more specific details. He said you can build different things with Legos, but not what those things are." The class started suggesting some revisions, and I jotted some down.

Legos

(page 1) **Have you ever felt bored? If you have, playing with Legos can help!** This book will teach about Legos.

(page 2) Legos are a toy that people build with. **They are rectangular bricks that come in lots of colors.** You can build lots of things with them **like spaceships, houses, and trains.**

(page 3) Kids and adults can both build with Legos. Babies shouldn't play with Legos.

LINK

Push writers to study their own folder full of writing, finding ways they can make their writing better. Ask them to put big Post-its on their writing wherever they see reasons to revise.

"Writers, can you take one of your own books out of your folder? You'll also see some Post-its in your folder. Take those out as well. As you start to read your writing, take aim at what we know makes for great information writing. Find places that need revision and mark those places with a Post-it. I bet you'll have revision Post-its on almost every page of each book."

After a moment, I said, "You can go to your work spots. Keep finding places to revise and then get started!"

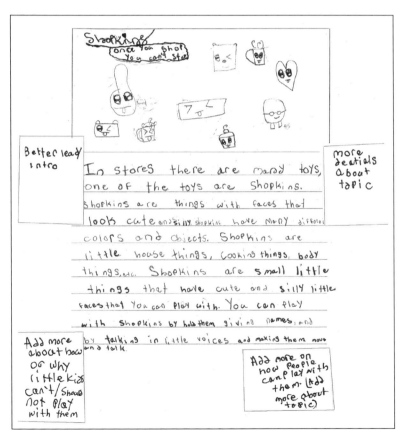

FIG. 6–1   One of this student's goal Post-its is to "Add more about how or why little kids can't/should not play with them."

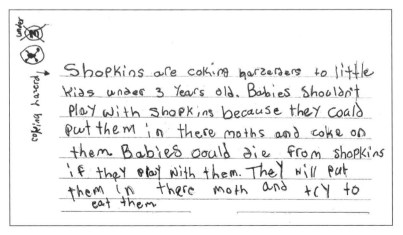

FIG. 6–2   The powerful revision resulting from the goal Post-it.

Support Students to Increase Volume, Produce Good Information Writing, and Comb New Learning through Revisions

TIME AND AGAIN, when Teachers College Reading and Writing Project organizes a walk-through of effective writing workshop classrooms, and when we meet afterwards to ask people who visited those rooms for one piece of next-step advice they'd give to the teacher, the Project staff and the visitors settle on one suggestion: the kids need to write more. If there is a second suggestion that comes close, it's that kids need to be encouraged to initiate revision. Our suggestion to you now is: don't wait for others to walk through your room. You can study your own class and chances are good you'll conclude the same thing.

Your students will probably have produced at least three information books by now. Actually, it's not the number of books so much as the number of pages that matters. Above all, look to see if your students are producing a lot more writing in one sitting now than they were at the start of this unit. If instead you see that your writers' books tend to have the same number of pages and lines now as at the beginning, then you'll want to gather a group together, tell them they need to amp up their volume of writing, and get them started, writing a ton, sitting side by side. Remind kids that one way to add information is by answering "Who, What, Where, and Why" questions on every page of their writing. Decrease expectations for quality if you need to do so to get your students producing longer pieces of writing (more pages, more lines).

Next, see if their writing has the basic characteristics that you have repeatedly supported. Is the writer teaching lots of information about one topic? Is the writer's book filled with details and facts about the topic? Does it seem as if the writer worked to make a special introduction? Does the writer seem to have made an effort to make each page special in some way?

Once you have checked to see that kids are beginning to produce writing that fits the characteristics of good information writing, you will want to study your children's writing process, especially their revision. In earlier sessions, we suggested you support revision by giving kids revision strips and sticky notes that help them add to an underdeveloped draft. What matters more than these tools is that you make revision itself appealing, and that you have a way to scan your students' work to see that they are revising on their own initiative. If a child has written three information books and when writing the fourth, you teach that child to work on his or her introduction, you will want to see that writer returning to each of his or her earlier books to revise the introductions in those books as well. The progression in this unit is that as kids write more texts, they learn more—and then they need to comb in the new learning and revise their stack of already-written books. This won't happen unless you champion it. Doing so gives the child exponentially more practice with all that you teach.

MID-WORKSHOP TEACHING   Enlisting Partners to Make Information Writing Even Better

"Can I have your eyes up here for a moment? I see your books are filled with Post-its marking places that you're aiming to improve. Many of you have even begun to make those improvements. Bravo!" I walked toward the "What Makes for Great Information Writing?" chart we had created.

"Will you give a thumbs up if you've revised your beginning to make sure that it is special?" I touched the first item. "Wonderful. Now, signal if you revised so that you teach a *lot* about your topic, including facts or numbers." Again students signaled and I began to move to the next items on the chart.

"Writers, you don't need *me* to move you through the items one by one on this chart. That's work you already know and do with your partner. Take the next minute or two to check in with your partner on the ways you are making your information writing great." Writers leaned in and began to study their drafts together as I circled the room complimenting and coaching.

① Nicholas

Marvels univers

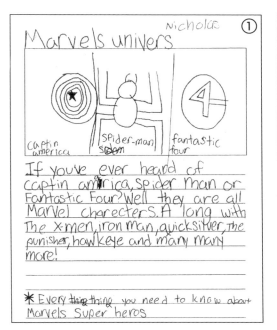

captin america | spider-man spdem | fantastic four

If you've ever heard of captin amrica, spider man or Fantastic Four? Well they are all Marvel charecters. A long with The X-men, iron man, quicksilver, the punisher, hawkeye and many many more!

* Every thing you need to know about Marvels super heros

②

All of these super hero's and vilens have specile abilitys. some are super stregth, super speed, Flight, teliportaion, Frezz breath, heat vison and much more! some just have wepons and gadgets like guns, knifes, sowrds, bow and arows, claws and more! some don't even have wepons!

③

Layers

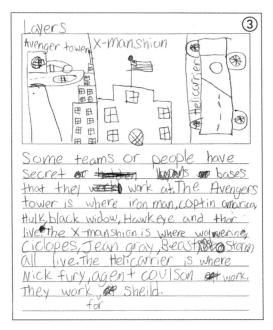

Avenger tower X-manshion Helicarrier

Some teams or people have secret or bases that they work at. The Avengers tower is where iron man, coptin amarica, Hulk, black widow, Hawkeye and thor live. The X-manshion is where wolverine, ciclopes, Jean gray, Beast, Storm all live. The Helicarrier is where Nick fury, agent coulson work. They work for sheild.

④

Movies

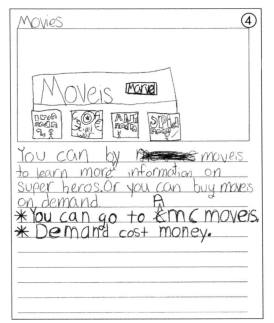

You can by moveis to learn more information on super heros. Or you can buy moves on demand.
* You can go to AMC moveis.
* Demand cost money.

⑤

The Avengers

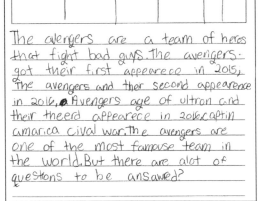

The avengers are a team of heros that fight bad guys. The avengers got their first appearece in 2015, The avengers and ther second appearence in 2016, Avengers age of ultron and their theerd appearece in 2016 captin amarica cival war. The avengers are one of the most famouse team in the world. But there are alot of questions to be ansawed?

⑥

Heros never cought on film

* The collector
* Shocker
* wasp
* spider-women
* carnage

You can watch every mavel movie you will not find them at all!

FIG. 6–3   Nicholas' third Bend I book

Provide Writers with a Sneak Peek of the Celebration

Gather your writers in the meeting area and explain that today's share is different.

"I thought we might do something a little different today for our share. This bend is coming to an end in just two more days. Instead of looking back over the work we've done in today's workshop, I thought we might look forward and think about this question: How will we celebrate our progress as information writers?" I paused for ten seconds, letting the writers consider this question.

"Last night my friend Ken sent me a video clip. Can I share it with you? I think we might find an answer to our celebration question by watching this video. It's a special kind of video called a TED Talk. As you watch it, consider if something about it reminds you of the work we've been doing this past week." I cued the video to 1:35 and pressed play. I stopped at 2:30.

"Writers, nod if you noticed that a TED Talk is a kind of information book, only on a stage instead of on paper. Let's test our theory. Could you tell your partner what Thomas taught about how to make an app? Try it."

After listening for about thirty seconds I said, "I heard you say that Thomas taught you that to make an app, you need to study a programming language like Java. He also taught some of you that iPhones come with a software development kit. But most of all, he taught you it costs $99 to get an app on the Apple app store! Thomas didn't just get up on stage and start talking. He anticipated questions the audience would have, and he included the answers in his teaching. Could we celebrate our information writing by staging our own TED-style talks?" A buzz of excitement filled the meeting area.

"Writers, I love this idea. I think we've found a way to celebrate ourselves as information writers."

If you are not familiar with TED Talks, we encourage you to check them out online. They are five to eighteen minutes long and each one is devoted to a fascinating topic—how body language shapes how you feel; great leadership; the power of vulnerability; the astonishing world under the sea. We recommend this particular TED Talk because it is delivered by a student rather than an adult. It should make the idea of TED Talks feel accessible to children.

WORKING WITH ENL STUDENTS

This session is already very supportive for ENLs:

◆ This minilesson and the "What Makes for Great Information Writing" chart synthesize all the teaching in this bend.

◆ Partners work together to study a clear example of great information writing.

◆ Students have many opportunities to practice looking for and adding in the qualities of strong information writing.

To provide additional support for ENLs, you might:

◆ Swap the darts analogy to a game that is more familiar to your students, such as soccer, or alternatively, act out throwing darts.

◆ Support repeated practice by coaching writers to comb revisions across pages and across books.

◆ Allow multiple viewings of Thomas's TED Talk in the share. Turning on the English subtitles provides additional exposure to print.

Editing for Run-On Sentences

IN THIS SESSION

TODAY YOU'LL teach students that one way writers prepare to publish is to reread their writing, looking for run-on sentences. They add punctuation to make their writing easier to read.

TODAY STUDENTS will reread and edit all of their information books. Expect to see them editing for *all* of the items on the editing checklist, including run-on sentences. Don't expect that they'll be able to recopy their drafts into perfect pieces for publication.

GETTING READY

✔ Display three run-on sentences for students to practice correcting (see Teaching).

✔ Print copies of a page with three additional run-on sentences, one per partnership (see Active Engagement).

✔ Prepare to display the "New and Improved Editing Checklist" and make small copies to distribute (see Link and Share).

✔ Display the "Why Information Authors Use Punctuation" chart (see Mid-Workshop Teaching).

✔ Today's minilesson video:

hein.pub/UTLINFO_7

MINILESSON

Editing for Run-On Sentences

CONNECTION

Make a case for editing conventions by stressing that presentation matters—in life, as in writing.

"Writers, this morning, before I came to school, I didn't just roll out of the house in my pajamas, with breakfast stuck in my teeth, and run straight here. I washed and brushed and flossed and combed and got dressed. I checked my look in the mirror. I made sure I was . . ." I smoothed a hand down the front of my shirt, "*presentable*.

"No matter how kind or smart I am *inside*, if I look all sloppy on the outside, people will judge me. It doesn't sound fair but it's true.

"It's equally true of your writing. You may have the most spectacular ideas and the most breathtaking information. But if your writing has no breaks, no paragraphs," I began counting out typical offenders, "if your words are sloppily spelled, if you don't add quotation marks around a quote, your reader will judge you. In fact," I feigned horror, "they might look at the page—and decide it's too difficult to read on. Just as it is important to package and present yourself to the world in your best light, it is important to present your *writing* to the reader in its best light."

❖ **Name the teaching point.**

"Today I want to teach you that writers reread their work looking out for parts that are hard to read, like two or three sentences that are squished together, pretending to be one sentence. When they find that—what writers call a run-on sentence—they add punctuation to divide that run-on sentence into smaller sentences that readers can understand."

TEACHING

Rally students to read some run-on sentences with you, noting with a partner what needs fixing. Think aloud about how you break those longer sentences into manageable chunks for readers.

"Let me show you what I mean. I have some sentences here that I've collected from past students. Get ready to look at each sentence with your partner and figure out if something needs fixing."

◆ COACHING

This is meant to be a bit silly. Ham it up!

Just a note. Paragraphing, it turns out, is especially important in information writing. You'll see we revisit that topic often in this unit.

I placed this sentence under the document camera:

> Mario is old but still popular it was made by Nintendo more
> than thirty years ago.

"That looks like a perfectly punctuated sentence. It starts with a capital letter and ends with a period . . . but hang on! Talk with your partner if you notice a problem." I gave partners just a moment to speak.

"Aha! I heard you say it looks like one sentence, but actually, there are *two* sentences squished together, trying to make you think it's one. What would you do with a sentence like this?" Students clamor to tell me to place a period after the word *popular*.

"Okay, that one was easy to spot. But look at this next one. Don't be fooled by that capital letter at the beginning and the period at the end. Read inside the sentence . . .

> Dogs are called man's best friend for a reason human
> friends sometimes fight a dog will never fight with you a
> dog will never get mad at you.

"I heard someone say there are more than two sentences squished inside here. Three? Wow, four? Call out where the periods should go." As children called out suggestions, I took a pen and placed periods where they belonged and then reread the sentences, this time making my voice pause at the right places.

"Sentences that go on and on like this are called *run-on sentences*. See why? Often a sign you have a run-on sentence is that you use the words *and* or *so* or *then* almost like Scotch tape to hold all the parts together. Look at this one."

> Dribble the ball away from the other player and look at the
> net and straighten your knees and jump slightly forward
> and push the ball upward and shoot.

"Can you find the Scotch-tape word? How would you fix this sentence?" I listened in and nodded, "You're right, there are too many *ands*. How many? Whoa, four *ands* in one sentence? Let's take some Scotch-tape *ands* out and break that sentence up."

Reiterate your teaching point, stressing that run-on sentences are hard on a reader's eyes.

"You learned earlier this year that it is important to avoid being rude as a writer. Just as it is rude to show up somewhere unbrushed and in pajamas, it's rude to give your reader writing that is full of sentences that run on and on and on. Be considerate. Make sure your reader's eyes don't have to work so hard to figure out where to stop."

ACTIVE ENGAGEMENT

Set students up to edit some typical run-on sentences.

"I'm going to pass around this paper with three sentences that look perfectly punctuated—until you read closely. See if you can problem solve these. Partner 1, read aloud the sentences. Partner 2, stop your partner at points where punctuation should be added. See if there's a Scotch-tape word you need to remove." I distributed a copy of three run-on sentences to each partnership.

> 1. If you need to change your baby brother's diaper first get wipes and you will also need a clean diaper and you will need rash cream and make sure you wash your hands after.
>
> 2. Pasta takes many fun shapes you have elbow-shaped and straight you even have corkscrews and bowtie pasta they all taste good.
>
> 3. Skateboards are not just a toy they are serious anyone can learn to skateboard you just need to practice don't be afraid to fall you will fall and you may even bleed it is a part of learning.

As children worked, I coached in.

- "Find the Scotch-tape word and cross it out."

- "Read it aloud. Where would you pause? That's where you'd put a period!"

- "Those look like too many thoughts to put down in one sentence. Break it up."

The language choices throughout this session are meant to be a bit playful. Enjoy.

The point of this is not for kids to get these right. Your bigger aim is to draw deliberate attention toward punctuation and hope that children become proactive in catching their own run-on sentences. You can, of course, decide to make these easier or harder. You can also make the work easier by reading these blurbs aloud for kids. But decreasing the challenge level of the work may not be advisable.

LINK

Channel kids to look for run-on sentences in their own writing, looking with the eyes of a stranger. Remind them to edit for everything on the editing checklist, not just for run-on sentences.

"Writers, in a second, I'm going to ask you to go back and look again at your own writing, with a stranger's eyes. You'll certainly want to check for run-on sentences, looking for places where your sentences go on and on, or where you use words like *and* and *so* and *then* a bunch of times. But remember, you'll be checking your pages—every page of every book—for not just run-on sentences, but for everything else on your editing checklist as well," and I revealed "The New and Improved Editing Checklist."

"Remember the checklist that we used in the narrative unit? I've brought that back, but now I call this the 'New and Improved Editing Checklist' because it has 'No more run-ons!' in it.

"Off you go to get your books reader ready!"

New and Improved Editing Checklist	
End sentences with punctuation. (. ! ?)	o ! ?
Begin each sentence with a capital letter.	There is a bear.
Spell using all you know about how words work.	snōw blōw knōw
Make sure others can read your writing.	
Check for run-on sentences.	STOP

Support Self-Editing

AS YOU MOVE ABOUT THE ROOM CONFERRING, remember that your students have written three information books in this bend, and you will want to use encouraging comments to help them self-edit all three books.

SMALL GROUP

Channel kids to divide their writing into paragraphs.

- "You've written a *ton*—whoa! But I worry that the reader's eye might get tired with no paragraph breaks. Let me get you some scissors, so you can cut this apart and separate the different parts. Will you read this and show me which part teaches one thing? Okay—so that part becomes the first paragraph. This other part, then, becomes a second paragraph."

- "Remember how, when you wrote stories, you started a new paragraph when the setting changed or a new character spoke? In information writing, the rule is to start a new paragraph when you teach something new. Reread your words and use the paragraph symbol to revise."

Hold writers accountable to using their best spellings.

- "I'm surprised that you misspelled the sight word *because*. Spelling is tricky when you're writing fast. Slow down for a minute and reread, circling all the words that feel misspelled and try fixing them. If you need to check the spelling, use the computer dictionary."

- "I'm impressed that you've used mature vocabulary in your piece. Like this word ____. When it's a long word, writers try to break it up into syllables to make sure they aren't skipping important letters in the spelling. Try breaking up this word and sound out each syllable."

Encourage peers to help each other to edit.

- "I've been admiring the collaborative work that happens at this table. You've really supported each other through the writing process. Don't stop now—help each other edit! It's always easier to see someone else's edit errors than to see our own. Exchange papers and edit away."

Remind students to use a variety of punctuation marks.

- "Try reading your writing out loud and listen to how your voice changes, especially for punctuation like periods, exclamation points, question marks, and quotation marks. Try it now. Read your piece out loud and listen for places where your voice stops or changes."

"Readers, eyes up here! You are really taking the work of reading your writing like a stranger seriously. How many of you have already found some run-on sentences and fixed them? Impressive!

"Periods aren't the only kinds of punctuation marks writers use. You know from our narrative unit that writers also use periods, question marks, exclamation marks, ellipses, and commas. Writers, check this out. I updated our 'Why Authors Use Punctuation' chart. Turn and tell your partner what you notice." I paused as the students studied the revised chart and pointed out the changes to their partners.

"Nice observations, writers. You noticed 'information' was added to the title of the chart and you noticed that the examples came from the piece on libraries. Remember, as you continue editing today, keep in mind all the different punctuation marks information writers can use, and choose your punctuation purposefully!"

Why Information Authors Use Punctuation

Punctuation mark	Authors use it to . . .	Example from 'Libraries'
Period: •	• make a statement • get readers to stop their voice	Usually librarians are ready to help you.
Question mark: ?	• ask a question • get readers to read it like a question with curiosity	Do you want to know ways that they are similar?
Exclamation mark: !	• show strong feelings • get readers to read with intensity	Then, keep reading!
Ellipses: • • •	• show characters thinking • get readers to stretch out pauses	Most towns have schools, police stations, a flag pole . . . and of course, a library.

Writing Partners Are Editors

Channel students to listen as a new reader reads aloud their piece, watching for places where that reader struggles. Remind writers that those are places where they should fix up their writing.

"Writers, come to the rug with your folder of work, and sit next to your partner." After partners had gathered, I said, "It's that time in our writing process when we need our checklists." I distributed small copies of the "New and Improved Editing Checklist" chart to each student.

"Would you and your partner work together to look between the items on this list and your writing? Give your work a quick 'editing test'—do your sentences begin with a capital letter and end with punctuation? Are the hard words spelled as best you can? Can others read your writing?

"Make sure your writing is as clear as it can be. You'll have more time to do this tomorrow, but get started now."

WORKING WITH ENL STUDENTS

This session is already very supportive for ENLs:

◆ You provide specific word clues such as *and* or *so* or *then* to help students find and fix run-on sentences.

◆ Students can practice the teaching point across the minilesson. You demonstrate it three times in the teaching and then writers practice with partners during the active engagement.

◆ This session provides a link between new learning and old. Students revisit the editing checklist as well as the varying ending punctuation chart, both familiar from the narrative unit.

To provide additional support for ENLs, you might:

◆ Lead a small group to offer extra support on breaking up writing into paragraphs.

◆ Make a "Before and After" T-chart comparing "before" sentences (run-ons) with "after" sentences to show how writing with more sentences looks different and is easier to read than run-ons.

Presenting Your Work
in Celebration

ᗡear Teachers,

The big day of celebration is here! Today should feel like a big deal—it is, after all, the culmination of seven days of your students' hard work and of *your* hard work. Your students rose to the challenge of becoming information writers and produced three information books in just over a week.

Today you will help students celebrate their information writing by letting them participate in a TED-like talk event. You will have already set them up for this celebration in the share of Session 6. Our idea is that today, you will give each of your students some time to present his or her topic to the group.

You might consider filming these TED-like talks and have students watch the video clips on the day of celebration. Although filming can be time-consuming and have the added burden of negotiating technology, getting ready to film their own work can also lend a burst of energy and investment to the group. So, it's up to you. Whether you arrange for a TED-like talk conference with presentations in person or by video recording, you'll want to be sure students are ready.

To get ready for today, you'll want each student to choose one of the information books he or she has written over the past few days to present.

You'll also want to give them some tips on presenting well. You might rewatch the clip of Thomas's TED Talk (www.ted.com/talks/thomas_suarez_a_12_year_old_app_developer#t-212182 search terms: Thomas Suarez app). As a reminder, the original clip you watched was from 1:35 to 2:30.

As kids watch, suggest that they think about what Thomas does to present well and that they make a list of what seems important to do when you present. The "To Present Well" chart lists items students might name and notice.

Then you can send off students in partnerships to practice presenting and giving each other tips. After about ten minutes of rehearsal, reconvene your writers and explain to them that there will be four different "stages" (for four audiences) in the classroom. This is just like the real TED Talks, where different speakers present on different stages. To make the event feel extra special, you could prepare tickets labeled *Stage One*, *Stage Two*, etc. Tell your students that in a moment you will hand them a ticket. That ticket will indicate where they will be presenting, as well as learning. After handing the writers their tickets, invite them to head to their stage.

You might decide to invite guests and set students up to present in small groups, with visitors watching each of the small groups. Students can present their talk and then they can take a few questions from visitors. If you decide to allow this, you might advise speakers to announce that they can take no more than two (or even one) questions.

After the students in the small groups finish presenting, you might reconvene the class and let them talk for a few minutes about what they have learned about information writing and how they feel they have become stronger writers. Visitors will no doubt be fascinated to hear about the insights students now have on this important genre. A sparkling apple juice toast to a job well done can add to the festivity. You might have students jot some of these reflections down and display these, along with their start-of-the-unit piece, to show the journey. And of course, you'll want to help students add their books to the classroom library, perhaps by making a basket of their books or by placing books written on topics you already have in the library, together with those other books. Encourage writers to check out and read books by their peers! You might even swap baskets with another class so that peers across a grade can read each other's information books during reading workshop time.

One note: in Bend III, students will each choose a book from Bend I to revise and improve, drawing on all that they will have learned across the unit up to that point. You may see students choosing to revise this book that they have presented today or another book they wrote during this bend. It is therefore essential that you keep the Bend I books close by so that your students can revisit them in the last part of the unit.

Know that your students will encounter the need to write informational pieces many times in their academic and professional careers, and in this unit, you have helped them to establish solid foundations in the work. They leave more equipped to do this kind of writing well.

So, celebrate, glory in the accomplishments of your student—and yourselves.

Cheers!
Lucy, Shana, and Hareem

> ## To Present Well
> - Speak loudly and clearly
> - Make eye contact
> - Use gestures
> - Keep some notes in your hand to refer to
> - Show visuals to help people understand (point to parts of your writing)

Bend II: Writing Chapter Books that Teach with Organization and Detail

There are two skills that matter especially to writers of information texts—organization and elaboration. This section of your unit focuses primarily on organization. It does this by inviting writers to plan the table of contents for their book and for each chapter within the book. It also encourages writers to think about how the page layouts can advance their messages—and to take paragraphing seriously. Toward the end of the bend, you point out that writers subtract information as well as add it. That subtraction occurs as writers reread to check that the sentences in each of their paragraphs fit together.

You start the bend by inviting students to each write a chapter book on a topic of personal expertise. They will plan and jot a table of contents page and divide their topic into logical subtopics. Teach the table of contents in such a way that your students jot quick lists of half a dozen chapters—there is no benefit from your students working for half an hour on this list! For those who want to make their book plans especially good, they should keep in mind that the chapter sequence is often logical. A book on seasons is more apt for its chapters to go in sequence—spring, summer, fall, and winter—than to jumble this sequence. The notion that an information text needs to have a logical structure will be revisited in the Units of Study books themselves, and your students will encounter this again as their proficiency progresses. The most important message is that writers divide their topics into subtopics. They plan to put all the information related to one subtopic in one place and the information for another subtopic in another place.

Your hope is that it takes students about fifteen minutes to write their tables of contents so that on the first day of this bend, they also have time to write one of their chapters. Let them know they can start with any chapter—and usually writers begin with the chapter they know best. The only chapter that won't work is their introduction or their closing. It would be terrific if you can provision your students with brads for securing the pages of their books together in a way that is completely flexible. This will allow them to order and reassemble their chapters in proper order later on.

Helping children choose the best paper for the first few pages of their books will be important. Look at the amount of writing those youngsters produced in a day during Bend I, and channel them to paper that has more lines than the amount of writing they produced in that bend. Make sure that the paper itself conveys a "write more" message to each writer. This is a very big deal. You won't get to all your kids before they choose paper for today's chapter, but know that through the next few days, your conferences can suggest that kids graduate to more sophisticated, demanding paper.

It is also important that students write on one side of the paper only so they can cut pages apart and repaste specific sections when they want to add information into specific sessions of a revised draft.

The mid-workshop teaching point in the first session of this bend is important—if need be, make it into a new session. Emphasize to your students that just as they can plan the sequence of chapters across their entire book, they can also plan the sequence of subtopics for any chapter. It can help to sketch those subtopics down the margins of their chapter pages to make a road map of the subtopics they plan to address. For example, if one chapter in a class book on Kid Injuries is titled "Kinds of Injuries," that chapter might begin with a section (and therefore a margin sketch) on scraped knees, and then it might progress by the end of the chapter to a section (and a sketch) on broken bones.

In the example above, having sketched a bunch of subtopics, the writer can use these sketches as a place to brainstorm the content for the chapter (and how much approximate space each subtopic will warrant). The writer who starts with scraped knees and ends with broken bones is also sequencing those subtopics so they go from small injuries to bigger ones. You'll want to adjust your teaching based on the proficiency level of your students—if they are more proficient, you'll want to highlight how logical structure matters. The writer doesn't just sketch subtopics to brainstorm more things to add. This is also a place to think, "What comes first, and why? What comes next, and why? How else could I sequence these subtopics?"

After their work in Bend I, your students will be accustomed to alternating between drafting a book and revising that book. In this bend that rhythm will continue as they alternate between drafting *a chapter* or two and revising that chapter or two. On the third day of this bend, you'll remind students to draw on all they learned in Bend I to revise the chapter or two that they will have written by then. They can reread those chapters, asking "Who, What, Where, Why" questions to spur elaboration. Encourage them to use scissors to cut a page apart, if needed, so they add information where it belongs. Alternatively, your students can revise to make their beginnings more special—or to add specialness to many parts of their chapter(s).

Midway through this bend, you'll teach students that writers think about the optional designs for their chapter-paper. This minilesson underscores the emphasis you'll be giving throughout the bend on planning and organization. It also helps your students assume the role of being "professional writers," functioning as real authors do. Kids will be reminded that the best way to rehearse for information writing is to imagine teaching a specific kind of reader. For example, a book on video games would contain different content if it were written for children or for grandparents.

Toward the end of the bend, you will teach the essential skill of paragraphing. You will highlight how bucketing information and leaving white space on the page dramatically lifts the level of students' writing. In the share of this session, you'll give your students homework—to recopy their best chapter on clean paper—for the celebration.

You may have noticed that in all the Up the Ladder books we are ambivalent about whether it is more worthwhile for students to correct and recopy their publications—or to move on to the next kind of writing. One could make an argument for students correcting a few kinds of errors in a draft, then putting the draft aside so as to move on. But one could also make a case for the importance of students completing a presentable final draft! Remember that with its emphasis on volume, this unit has children writing five to six information books across three bends. You might choose to hold off on a bigger publishing celebration here and do that at the end of Bend III instead.

In the final session of this bend, you'll teach students how to give powerful feedback to each other. Writers will form celebration groups and read each other's writing like it's gold and compliment that writing in precise ways.

Organizing into Chapters

Planning in Preparation for Writing Chapter Books

IN THIS SESSION

TODAY YOU'LL teach students that once information writers have a topic, they organize their information and ideas into categories, which become individual chapters, parts, and paragraphs.

TODAY STUDENTS will create a table of contents for a new information book with chapters. They will then start to write any chapter they choose.

GETTING READY

✓ Display the "Topics for Information Writing" chart from Bend I (see Connection).

✓ Be ready to display the grocery images page for the sorting game (see Connection).

✓ Prepare to add to the "How to Write a Nonfiction Chapter Book" anchor chart (see Connection, Teaching, Mid-Workshop Teaching, and Share).

✓ Select a topic to write about for your class book. We model with "Kid Injuries" (see Active Engagement).

✓ Prepare blank booklets to distribute during the independent practice. Each booklet should start with a table of contents

page and contain just two to three other pages, because you'll soon channel students to add pages that have special formats. Use brads, not staples, to hold the pages together so that more pages can be added later. Make a hole at the top of each page for the brads. Each page (each chapter) must contain roughly as many lines as entire books from Bend I, since students will write a *chapter* a day, not a *book* (see Link).

✓ Select mentor nonfiction texts with a table of contents for students to study (see Conferring and Small-Group Work).

✓ Today's minilesson video:

hein.pub/UTLINFO_9

Organizing into Chapters
Planning in Preparation for Writing Chapter Books

CONNECTION

Rally students to a new bend and the new challenge of spending a week writing one chapter book. Help them settle on a topic for their book.

"Writers, the books you've written so far are so full of information that I think you are ready to take on the very grown-up project of writing nonfiction *chapter* books."

"To do this, you need to have a topic that you will teach others about. This needs to be a topic you know really well, because you won't just write a little book." I held up one of their information picture books. "Instead, you will be writing a whole *chapter* book on your topic. Think of the topics you know well, things you are famous for. Like you all know that *I* am crazy about dogs. This chart might give you some ideas." I put up the "Topics for Information Writing" chart from Bend I.

"So let's get our topics figured out. Tell kids sitting near you what *you* think they're famous for. Go!" I listened in as children talked, then I said, "I'm hearing that we have experts on cellphones and karate, visiting Mexico and SpongeBob. Right now, instead of talking, take a second to think quietly. Decide on the topic for your book." I left a pool of silence, then said, 'Whisper your topic to your partner."

"Hold your topic in your mind for a minute. Because you'll be writing a *looong* book, with tons of information, one of the most important things you will do is to organize. Thumbs up if you think you're good at organizing. I see lots of thumbs. I'm going to test you!"

◆ COACHING

There is probably nothing more important to this genre than organization. It is important at the macro level (when thinking about a whole book) and at the chapter level as well (when thinking about subtopics).

Resist the urge to channel students toward lofty topics like the UN or the Gold Rush. It may be tempting to think, "I'll kill two birds with one stone," channeling students to write about a social studies topic while also teaching this writing unit. Sometimes the result is two dead birds. Writing an information book with chapters will be challenging enough without students attempting topics they don't know well.

Play a quick sorting game to "test" children's organization.

"People who are good at organizing clean laundry make *a separate* pile for T-shirts. They match their socks and put rolled pairs in a *separate spot* in the drawer.

"I'm going to test your organizational talents with a game. I'll show you some groceries to organize. Which items would you store together? Work with a partner." I displayed the image.

After about ten seconds, I reconvened children and invited one partnership to share its idea. "Maria and Jacob, I heard you coming up with a great organizational plan."

Jacob spoke up: "We decided to divide these groceries into three kinds . . ."

"Three *categories?*" I nodded, supplying the academic word I hoped Jacob and the rest of the class would come to own.

Jacob restated, "Three categories. One for items that go in the fridge, like milk and vegetables. One for items in kitchen cabinets, like cans and cereal. Then stuff for the bathroom, like soap and toothpaste." I pointed out that another partnership had categorized by item types, like food and supplies, and another had categorized by color.

"You're all nodding in agreement! This game was easy for you. That bodes well for the writing you will be doing. For your big writing project this week, you won't be able to just think of a topic, then touch a page, and start saying what you'll write on that page." I started a new anchor chart and added the first two bullets. No way! You are going to need to *organize*."

❖ **Name the teaching point.**

"Today I want to teach you that information writers organize their information and ideas into categories. Those categories become separate chapters, parts, or paragraphs. When they are writing an information book, the first way they organize is by creating a table of contents."

TEACHING

Give kids repeated quick practice at imagining several different possible ways that a table of contents could go for a few subjects they know well.

"To practice thinking about a topic for a book and the categories or chapters you might include, imagine you are writing a book on the seasons. Tell your partner one way the table of contents—also known as a TOC—could go." I let kids talk, and commented on how I loved the way many used their fingers as an organizer. "How about a book on school?" I asked. "Tell the person beside you how it might go!"

Again the room broke into a hubbub. I called kids back and said, "I heard different ways that a book on school could go. On the one hand," I said, holding up a hand, "the chapters could be math, science, reading, writing." Holding up a different hand, I said, "Or kindergarten, first grade, second grade.

"My point, writers, is this. When you write a longer nonfiction book, it helps to think of different possible ways your chapters might go, and then to write a table of contents that goes with the plan you choose."

ACTIVE ENGAGEMENT

Recruit students to help you devise a table of contents for what will become a class book on children's injuries.

"Let's practice this work together so you can build your categorizing muscles," I flexed my biceps. "Let's write another book together. I've heard you all talking a lot about all the ways you've gotten hurt. Broken bones, sprained ankles. My goodness. You know a lot about injuries. What if . . . we write a book on 'Kid Injuries'? Are you game?" The kids nodded, wiggling with pleasure.

"Let's start with a blank book—one with just a few pages for now. We can add pages later." I picked up a blank book with three pages. "Let's start with a table of contents page. What do we do first? We need to sort the laundry!"

"I'm sort of joking, but just as we organize our clean clothes by category before we put them away (T-shirts, socks, shorts)—when we plan our table of contents, we have to figure out what our piles of information will be. We won't have chapters called "T-shirts" and "Socks"—but what *will* our chapters be?" I added, "I don't know how this book could go, so I am relying on you."

Students were quiet. The buzz of activity that I had anticipated was not happening. "Whenever I am feeling uncertain about my ideas, I give myself permission to be uncertain by beginning with the word *Maybe*. Try this." I voiced over, "*Maybe* one chapter might be . . . *Maybe* another chapter could be . . .

To get kids thinking structurally, give them multiple opportunities to divide a topic into parallel subtopics. You might generate a few other quick examples. To write about dogs, you could write about retrievers, spaniels, and terriers. To write about a library, you might write about fiction, nonfiction, and reference books. This is quick. They don't need to discuss this for too long or come up with a perfect TOC. They just need to get the idea of dividing a topic into parallel subtopics.

You may notice that we aren't suggesting a book on school might have a hodgepodge of math and science chapters intermixed with chapters on kindergarten and fifth grade. Your examples should probably have a logical order.

Although you could use an alternate topic here, we recommend that you use the book topic we've provided. Choosing an alternate topic will require you to alter most of the upcoming sessions, as this book topic threads throughout the bend. If you choose another topic, it should be one that you and the kids can coauthor. Think of this more as a class book than a personal book.

The book you hold up can be the size of a kid's book, if you have a way to project and enlarge the page. If not, you might want to make it out of chart paper. Look ahead, however, to Session 12 and think about how you'll make chart paper "pages" that are described in that minilesson.

When you listen in on kids' talk and then convene the class to say, "Let me share what I heard," you can tweak what you heard so you report on what you wish *you had heard. If you don't get ideas like these from your kids, you can either say you did, or you can say, "Your ideas got me thinking of another chapter or two. What about a chapter on . . ." and then suggest any chapters you didn't hear the kids mentioning.*

"Can you get into groups of four or five, sitting right where you are? Using your hand as an organizer, come up with how the chapters might go in a book on kid injuries." Soon the room was buzzing with categories. I moved from group to group, adding my own ideas to their suggested table of contents.

After a few minutes, I reconvened the writers and projected two new drafts of a possible table of contents page. "Writers, take a look at the categories or chapters that I've heard you suggest for our class information book on kid injuries. Think and decide if one TOC seems good to you."

Two Ways Tables of Contents Could Go on the Class Topic

Kid Injuries		Kid Injuries	
CONTENTS		CONTENTS	
Broken bones	1	Kinds of kid injuries	1
Scraped knees	2	Getting help	2
Chipped Teeth	3	Fixing kid injuries	3
		Staying safe	4

We steered kids toward the second TOC, because the subcategories within those chapters would be clearer, more obvious. We encourage you to follow the second plan, or a variation of it. You can act as if it came from overheard partner conversations.

LINK

Rally writers to think of several ways their tables of contents could go. Once they have shared some possibilities, channel them to write them on special table of contents paper.

"Writers, the work we just did is the work each of you needs to do on your own. Ask yourself what *your* piles of information will be. Remember, it's okay to say, 'Maybe one chapter will be . . .' and 'Maybe another chapter will be . . .' Turn and talk to your partner about how you might divide your topic into smaller parts."

After children talked, I said, "Today, start by working on a table of contents for your book. Each booklet on your table starts with a table of contents page. The table of contents is sort of like the schedule for our day, only it is the schedule for the topics in your book. You'll probably plan about five chapters, even though your books don't have that much paper yet. The table of contents should just take about five minutes, and after that, start writing one of your chapters. Off you go!"

Before sending the class off to write, be sure that you have put booklets on the tables. While kids once wrote a book a day, now they'll be writing one or two chapters a day, so if the books once contained four or five lines a page, the chapters need to contain more like fifteen lines per page. For kids who may attempt several tables of contents, you might make single pages of this paper available.

Predictable, Quick Interventions to Keep the Whole Class Writing Up a Storm!

DURING TODAY'S WRITING TIME, you'll want to move quickly among your students, channeling them to work with energy and independence.

Match children to paper choice that challenges rather than overwhelms or underwhelms them.

When you equip kids with booklets, the number of lines on each page should be based on your expectations for each writer. You'll want the page itself to act as a sort of challenge for the writer, as if the page is calling "fill me up."

Expect that some kids won't understand the purpose of a table of contents. Be ready to redirect and coach.

You may find that some kids still might not grasp the concept that they are to write a whole book about one umbrella topic and that they should plan the whole book prior to writing anything else. They especially may not grasp that the table of contents is a listing of future chapter titles, with a space next to each chapter title to write the page number. You may want to gather a small group and coach them on how a table of contents works, showing them some examples in familiar information books.

Keep an eye out for volume.

Making a table of contents is not the work of an entire day. Rally kids to spend five minutes on this, then turn quickly to writing a chapter. Remind them to plan the chapter, perhaps quickly sketching some possible subtopics (on top of the chapter page, or along the margin) within any one chapter page. Plan on most of your kids completing at least one chapter, but don't be discouraged if that doesn't happen. The big job is to get them writing. Suggest they write *any* chapter—the one they know most about will be easiest. If books are held together with brads, kids can alter the order of the chapters later. Each chapter should be the writer's effort to teach readers everything that writer knows about that chapter's subtopics.

MID-WORKSHOP TEACHING   Making Plans for Writing: Using Key Words or Quick Sketches as Reminders

"Writers, by now you should have finished your TOC and started to write a chapter. Remember, you don't need to write Chapter 1 first. You can start with any chapter, whichever is easiest for you to write. Even if you start with Chapter 3, you can write it on that first chapter page in your book—the brads let you move pages around later.

"Remember to take thirty seconds to plan. One way is to jot key words or make tiny sketches down the margin of your page to remind yourself of what you want to say. You can see that I made a plan for a chapter on 'Kinds of Kid Injuries,' from little ones to big ones, so that first drawing is a knee with a Band-Aid. My sketch of a broken leg is at the bottom of my chapter page. You can take a jiffy to do the same, then get started writing!" I added a bullet to the anchor chart.

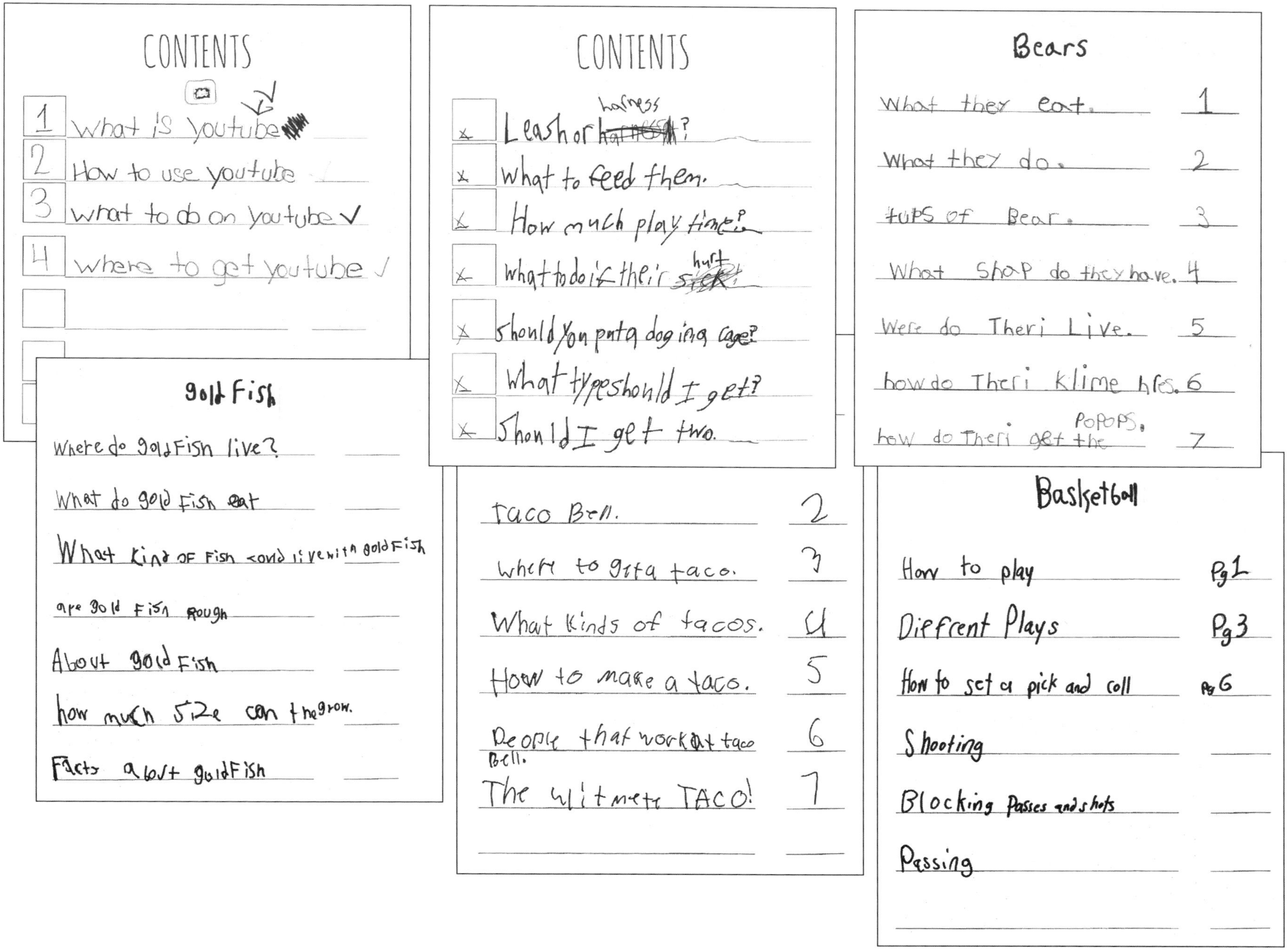

CONTENTS

1. what is youtube
2. How to use youtube
3. what to do on youtube ✓
4. where to get youtube ✓

CONTENTS

- x Leash or harness?
- x what to feed them.
- x How much play time?
- x what to do if their hurt sick
- x should you put a dog in a cage?
- x What types should I get?
- x should I get two.

---

gold Fish

where do goldFish live?

What do gold Fish eat

What kind of Fish could live with goldFish

are gold Fish Rough

About gold Fish

how much size can the grow.

Facts about goldFish

Taco Bell.   2

where to git a taco.   3

What kinds of tacos.   4

How to make a taco.   5

People that work at taco Bell.   6

The ultmete TACO!   7

Bears

What they eat.   1

What they do.   2

tips of Bear.   3

What shop do they have.   4

Were do Theri Live.   5

how do Theri klime hres.   6

how do Theri get the POPOPS.   7

Basketball

How to play   Pg 1

Diefrent Plays   Pg 3

How to set a pick and coll   Pg 6

Shooting

Blocking Passes and shots

Passing

FIG. 9–1 These Table of Contents work like organization plans for the writing that will follow.

A Chapter, Like a Book, Can (Sort of) Follow a Table of Contents

Teach writers to think whether they could make a table of contents for just one chapter.

"Writers, pause in your writing. Even if you're not done writing that chapter, will you reread it to yourself? As you do, think about what the table of contents could be *for that chapter*.

You won't actually write a TOC for each chapter. But here is the important thing—you should write each chapter so that you *could* make a table of contents for it, if you had to. Organizing and categorizing are just as important *within* a chapter as they are across a whole book.

"If your chapter is like jumbled laundry, use scissors or arrows to separate and sort the subtopics. If you haven't written enough to sort—use this time to write super-fast. Remember to start a new paragraph each time you begin a new subtopic."

WORKING WITH ENL STUDENTS

This session is already very supportive for ENLs:

◆ Students write on topics of personal expertise, allowing them to draw from and feel pride in their own extensive knowledge. It also celebrates the diverse areas of expertise in the classroom.

◆ Kids can again rehearse for their writing by teaching the topic to a peer.

◆ Students will be able to cycle back through the same writing process they have now experienced several times, this time working at a more sophisticated level. Building on similar work allows them to develop expertise and confidence.

◆ The grocery game gives students a chance to work in pairs using familiar visuals to understand the concept of organization.

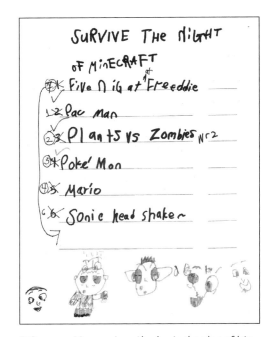

FIG. 9–2   Max revises the logical order of his chapters.

CONTENTS

ch 2. What Dogs Do

Dogs care about humans more than humans care about Dogs. Dogs Protect human even when they are old Dogs help People when they're Blind.

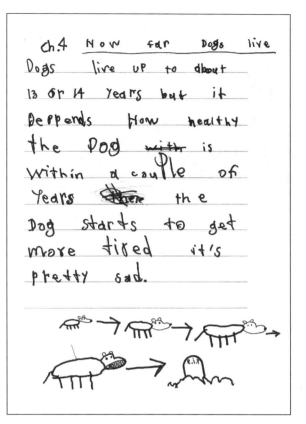

ch.4 How far Dogs live

Dogs live up to about 13 or 14 years but it Deppends How healthy the Dog ~~with~~ is Within a couple of years ~~back~~ the Dog starts to get more tired it's pretty sad.

FIG. 9–3   Eli ensures that each chapter contains content that is distinct.

Rehearsing for Writing by Teaching

IN THIS SESSION

TODAY YOU'LL remind students that information writers get ready to write by teaching (or pretending to teach) their topic, thinking, "How can I especially interest this particular student/reader?"

TODAY STUDENTS will write another chapter or two of the information book they started yesterday.

GETTING READY

✔ Prepare to add to the "How to Write a Nonfiction Chapter Book" anchor chart (see Teaching Point and Link). 👆

✔ Choose a chapter from the class book to demonstrate how to think about the audience when deciding upon content for a chapter. We model with "Getting Help" (see Teaching).

✔ Print out Sentence Starter cards, one for each pair of students in the small group (see Conferring and Small-Group Work). 👆

✔ Display the "What Makes for Great Information Writing?" chart (see Share). 👆

✔ Today's minilesson video:

hein.pub/UTLINFO_10

Rehearsing for Writing by Teaching

CONNECTION

Contextualize today's teaching by reminding kids that in the narrative unit, they learned to rehearse for writing by storytelling. Now they'll rehearse for information writing by teaching.

"Earlier, when writing narratives, you learned that just as a choir rehearses for a concert, story writers rehearse for their writing. They tell their story over and over to listeners, trying to make it better even before they put a word onto the page.

"Information writers also rehearse. As information writers, as nonfiction writers, you are writing to *teach* people, so one of the best ways for you to rehearse is by teaching your topic. If you can *teach* your topic well, you can *write it* well."

Connections often aim to connect today's teaching to yesterday's—or last unit's—prior work. That is what this connection is doing.

Ask students to select a chapter from their table of contents they will rehearse and draft today.

"Right now, will you choose a chapter you'll rehearse and draft today? If you haven't quite finished the chapter you started yesterday, leave it for now and get started on a new one. You can come back and finish that first chapter later. Either way, decide on what you will write today." I gave students a few seconds to decide. "Give me a thumbs up when you've settled on the chapter you'll write today."

If kids have their chapter in mind they'll find it easier to apply the learning of the minilesson. Expect kids to settle on topics quickly, and do not fret over whether every kid has made this choice. This portion of your minilesson should take only a few seconds.

❖ **Name the teaching point.**

"Today I want to emphasize that you can get ready to write a chapter by teaching the topic (or pretending to teach it). First, you think about who your readers—your students—will be and what will especially interest them. Then you teach (or pretend to teach) your topic. By doing this, you rehearse for your writing." I added the teaching point to our anchor chart.

TEACHING

Suggest that writers keep their audience in mind, varying the topic to keep the audience interested.

"A writer keeps the reader in mind just like a teacher keeps her students in mind. If I had to teach a class on new phone apps, I'd teach that class very differently depending on whether my students were kids like Edgar," I pointed at a kid in my room, ". . . or if I were writing it for my grandma!

"For you Edgar, I'd talk about apps that help with homework and research. To explain them, I might compare them to apps you already use. But my grandmother is totally new to phone apps, so if I were writing for a class of people like her, I'd start with basics and write in a step-by-step way. I might say, 'You can use apps to look at photos of your grandkids . . .'

"Writers, do you get my point? When I go to teach a topic, I think, 'Who are my students? What will make this topic interesting to them?'"

Model thinking about possible audiences for your topic, and thinking about what will interest each audience.

"Let's try this for our chapter, 'Getting Help.' To practice planning with an audience in mind, for now, let's imagine we are writing for *kids*: What will *kids* need to know about getting help with an injury?"

Students suggested kids would want to know that they should go to the school nurse if they're at school, or call an adult to help, or if it is a big emergency, even call 911. "Now let's think if we're writing for parents. What will parents want to know about getting help when their child is injured?"

The kids said parents would want to know if they should try fixing the injury at home, or if they should call the doctor, or if they should rush their child to the emergency room.

Name the work you demonstrated in a way that highlights what you hope kids will do often when they write.

"Do you see that for us to get ready to write a chapter, 'Getting Help,' we had to first think about our readers, our students? Then it was important to think, 'What will interest my reader about this topic?' That question can help us plan the different subtopics that we will write about in any one chapter. That will set us up to sketch or jot the subtopics we plan to write about in a chapter."

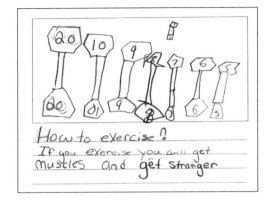

FIG. 10–1   A caption brings an illustration to life.

This repetition of the teaching point at different places in the lesson is entirely intentional. These are the words you want to imprint on children's minds, the words you want them to internalize as a go-to strategy whenever they write information texts, in your classroom and in the years and space beyond.

ACTIVE ENGAGEMENT

Ask students to first determine the audience for their book. Then have them rehearse their chapter, keeping in mind the information that will be particularly fascinating for their audience.

"It's your turn to try this. Think about your book, asking yourself, 'Who is this book for? Who are my readers?' Consider a few possibilities. Are you writing a book for your family? For the parents of other kids? For kids who are experts on this topic? For little kids who know nothing about the topic? For teachers? For kids in our class? Tell your partner who your audience will be." I gave partners just a moment or two to talk.

"Great! Now that you have your audience in mind, it's time to rehearse the chapter you'll write today. When you make a plan for your chapter, keep in mind the subtopics your audience will want to know."

"Ready to try it? Use your fingers to tell some of the subtopics you will write about in that chapter. Sketch or jot those down the margin of your page to remind yourself of subtopics.

"Before you sketch and write, rehearse by teaching that chapter to your partner. Include details that will fascinate your readers! Partners, as you listen, suggest other information that might fascinate readers."

After a minute and a half, I said, "Partners, will you switch roles? If you've been listening, now you should rehearse how you'll teach your chapter to your audience. Include details that will be super-interesting to your audience."

LINK

Explain that writers don't have to teach aloud to rehearse. They can teach in their minds. Send kids off to draft the chapter they rehearsed and, if they have time, to rehearse and draft another one.

"I can tell you're fired up and ready to draft this chapter you just rehearsed. In about a minute you'll head off to draft the whole chapter. But to rehearse for your writing, you don't actually need to teach. You can *pretend* to teach. You can teach in your mind.

"That might sound weird, but it's true. Even now, the way I get ready to teach a minilesson is I teach it first to the rear view mirror or the snowdrifts as I drive to school. My car has heard more minilessons than you can believe! That's because teachers teach 'in the air' before they teach real kids.

"I'm going to update our chart with today's new strategy. *And*, I am adding what you learned in Bend I about drafting and revising because you'll want to apply that to your chapter books."

"Off you go to draft this chapter and then rehearse and draft another one!"

Focus on Students Who Don't Begin to Write Right Away and Get Them Started

ON SOME DAYS IN THIS BEND, most kids will be drafting a chapter or two. The writers who write just one chapter in a day's workshop will hopefully be writing something roughly equivalent to a page of notebook paper. Other writers will use paper and write in chapters that are closer to half that length, and they may well write several chapters in a day's writing workshop. You may have kids whose writing is so slow that it seems as if they are inscribing marble. You might want to clarify expectations of length (but don't make those expectations too much out of their zone).

Rally a writer to write more by listening to him tell you a lot about his topic.

Sometimes you can rally a writer to write by inviting him or her to talk and showing utter absorption in the topic, oohing and ahhing in ways that will make him say more. Help the writer feel ownership and power connected to this topic. You might listen for two minutes and say, "I am blown away by what you know." Dictate back some of what he said, prompting him to add notes in the margins for where those words might go. The bit of text that a writer produces this way can do wonders for getting him started on writing a strong chapter.

Invite students to rehearse with partners.

Rehearsing before writing is a big deal. Pair kids up, and ask one to teach the other. As one writer talks through her topic, the listening partner might jot a few key words or sketch a few pictures down the margin of the writer's page, capturing different aspects of the subtopic that the rehearsing writer covers. That is, in the margin of a page about dog food, there could be a jotted word *breakfast*, and farther down the page, the word *lunch*.

SMALL GROUP

Help writers to use an imagined reader to help them say more about a topic.

To get ready, print Sentence Starter cards for each pair of students. Gather students on the rug, and set them up to work in pairs.

Tell the writers that you saw they were having a hard time coming up with things to say in their chapter, and help them know that thinking about a reader can help. Direct each writer to pick one sentence starter, say it aloud to his or her partner, and then say more about the topic.

Writers can each do that with two of the sentence starters. Then they write those sentence starters and what they said aloud into their chapter.

Send them back to their writing spots to continue this work independently. Give them a copy of the sentence starters to take along with them.

> ### Sentence Starters: Ways a Writer Can Talk to a Reader
>
> Do you want to know about . . .
>
> One big thing to know is . . .
>
> Another big thing to know is . . .
>
> You probably wonder . . . But . . .
>
> If you are wondering . . . The answer is . . .

"Writers, some of you are almost at the bottom of one page and on to the next. Way to go! If you aren't close to the bottom of a page, push yourself to write faster. How many of you remembered to start a new paragraph each time you started teaching a new subtopic inside your chapter?" Some signaled yes, while others looked down at their pages. "Start now! Mark where you plan to begin a new subtopic and remember to skip a line so that your reader's eye can follow your organization. Now

shake out your hand, rest up for a minute, and teach in your mind what you are going to write next."

I gave them a moment to think. "In a few seconds, we're going to have a ten-minute write-a-thon. That means ten minutes of nonstop writing, writing, writing. I'm going to time you. See how many lines you can get done in those ten minutes. Ready . . . set . . . go! Write up a storm."

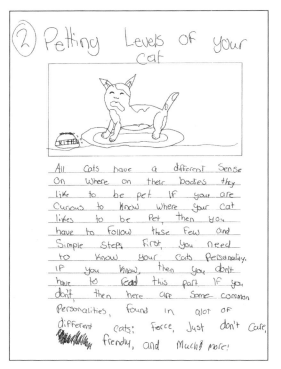
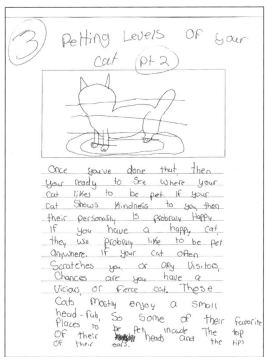
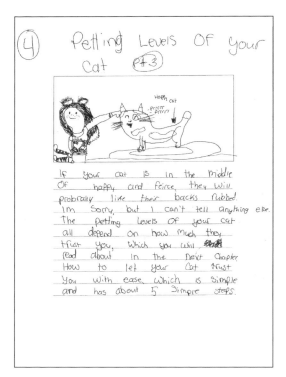

FIG. 10–2   Write-a-thons can result in multi-page chapters.

Taking Stock and Making Plans

Remind writers that while thinking of their readers and their topics, they should also keep in mind the qualities of good information writing. This will guide drafting—and revising.

"Writers, bring your books to the meeting area." I said, "Will you show your partner how much you wrote? Count the number of lines you wrote today!" After the children counted, I said, "Who wrote more than a page?" Thumbs went up, and I signaled that absolutely, that was the sort of volume I expected. "Who wrote twenty lines—or more?" Again, I nodded, affirming the writers. "If you didn't write that much today, push yourself tomorrow. You can't teach a lot if you don't write a lot."

Then I said, "But writing a lot is just one goal. You also want to write *well*. How many of you remembered to aim for a special beginning?" Some signaled yes, and I gave them a thumbs up. "It is hard to remember everything when you write—to think about your audience and your subtopics, as well as good writing. The good thing is that after you write, you'll get a chance to revise. Tomorrow you'll be revising the chapter you wrote today—actually, anything you have written so far.

"So let's end today by rereading and thinking about what we could do tomorrow to make our writing even better. Use our chart, 'What Makes for Great Information Writing?' to help you jot some Post-its to yourself about plans for how you can revise tomorrow—and partners, help each other." I put the "What Makes for Great Information Writing?" chart from Bend I front and center.

After a few minutes, I said, "Turn and tell your partner what you're thinking. You might say, 'Tomorrow I need to work on . . .' Leave yourself some Post-it notes, and reread any chapters you have written so far."

Partnerships burst into conversation to discuss writing goals.

WORKING WITH ENL STUDENTS

This session is already very supportive for ENLs:

◆ The session highlights how writers say (rehearse) what they'll write before actually writing it.

◆ Partnerships provide more opportunities to use the language structures of information writing.

◆ The conferring and small-group work provides "Ways a Writer Can Talk to a Reader" sentence starters, which scaffold the use of information book language.

To provide additional support for ENLs, you might:

◆ Create and reference a chart containing the list of questions, "Who is my audience? How can I make this topic interesting? What does this audience want to know?"

◆ Provide more turn-and-talk opportunities during the active engagement. Channel kids to try teaching one way as if addressing one audience, another way as if addressing another.

Writers Are the Bosses of Their Writing

IN THIS SESSION

TODAY YOU'LL teach students that writers draw upon all they know about writing and revising information books to set goals and take charge of their own writing.

TODAY STUDENTS will make a plan for the work they want to do. Some students may revise the chapters that they have written. Some students might draft another chapter.

GETTING READY

✔ Prepare a drafted chapter of your class book for demonstration. We use "Getting Help" (see Teaching).

✔ Display and prepare to add to the "How to Write a Nonfiction Chapter Book" anchor chart (see Teaching, Link, and Mid-Workshop Teaching).

✔ Write a new beginning for your chapter on a Post-it to show how you might revise (see Teaching).

✔ Today's minilesson video:

hein.pub/UTLINFO_11

Writers Are the Bosses of Their Writing

CONNECTION

Congratulate children for taking charge of rehearsing for writing. Then point out that some of them appeared unsure what to do once they started writing—that their confidence was gone.

"Writers, join me on the rug and bring your writing folder with Post-its and a pen with you."

When kids were seated, I said, "Yesterday, I told you that I often get ready to teach minilessons by teaching snowdrifts as I drive to school, and we laughed. But when it was time to write, I saw many of you rehearse for writing by teaching an imaginary class, a pile of books . . . even Hermie the Hamster! I loved watching how you took charge of rehearsing for writing.

"But then I noticed something else. Once you got to writing, some of you looked a bit unsure. All that confidence you'd had while teaching was gone. You looked around the room, as if wondering how to begin writing. Some of you even came up to me to ask what you should do next.

"I admit, writers, you threw me for a loop. It was as if my class of expert information writers had been replaced with kids who haven't been in a writing workshop all these months. So listen up close."

Name the teaching point.

"Today I want to remind you that professional writers don't line up beside a teacher and ask, 'What should I do? What should I do?' Writers know they are the bosses of their own writing, and *they decide* what their writing needs—and then, they do it!"

Prepare to return to this teaching point often. Each time a child comes to you with a question or problem that they could easily have solved without your help, shrug and say, "Writers are the bosses of their own writing. You decide what you ought to do!" And then compliment (or coach into) the decision they make, marveling at the independence they've just shown.

TEACHING

Channel kids to draw on one way of revising that they learned in Bend I—to imagine revisions they could initiate on a chapter in the class book. Emphasize that kids can make their own decisions.

"We've got a class book going—a book about getting help with kid injuries—so today we can practice being bosses of our writing by working on that book. Then I'm *hoping* you'll be game to spend this whole day just revising. And you know who would be the boss of those revisions?" The kids pointed to themselves, and I did as well. "That's right—you are!

"So let's practice making decisions about what a draft needs by working with the chapter we began the other day on the nurse's office and the hospital. Remember your suggestions for writing it as if the readers were parents?"

I placed the following "draft" under the document camera.

Getting Help

When kids get hurt at school, they almost always get help by going straight to the nurse's office. The nurse has a first aid kit. The nurse can stop the bleeding, and she can keep a huge bump from swelling too much. She can also check to see if something serious is going on.

If the kid needs stitches or X-rays or a cast, then the nurse usually calls the student's parent.

When a kid gets hurt BADLY, then the parent might get help by taking the kid to the emergency room. At the hospital, parents have to fill out a lot of forms. It can be a two-hour wait before the kid gets seen by a nurse or a doctor.

"Now we *could* run around saying, 'Our chapter's done. What do we do next? What do we do next?'" I leaned in closer as I reiterated the teaching point: "Or, *We* could decide to be the bosses of our own writing. To do that, we reread our writing, remembering what we know about how to draft and revise information writing." I moved those Post-its from our anchor chart front and center.

"Let's think about possible ways we could make our chapter better." I moved my finger to the first Post-it and said, "Remember this? Earlier we learned that if our writing is short and we want to add on, to elaborate, we can ask 'Who, What, Where, Why' questions to come up with more information. That's one option for revising our 'Getting Help' chapter. Let's think about other options." I ran my finger to the second Post-it—writing with specific details—and said, "Hmm, . . . Here's another thing we could do. We could write with specific details: colors, quotes, numbers . . ."

Draft and Revise.

• Think of the questions people will ask, and answer them.

Who..?   Where..?
What..?   Why..?

• Include specific details.

Numbers   Shapes   Sizes
Quotes   Colors   Names

• Aim to make a special beginning and ending.

Emphasize independent decision making by asking students to pick the specific strategy to revise this shared chapter.

"You could wait for *me* to tell you which of these two options you could use. *Or* you could act like the boss of this piece and come to your own decision about a way to improve our draft on 'Getting Help.'" I leaned forward. "You guys are pros. Go ahead. Decide. How will you revise this chapter?" I glanced down at my watch as if to time the kids.

After about ten seconds, I whispered, "Bosses, now that you've picked the strategy, make this revision in your head. In a bit, you'll have the chance to share the words you'd add on to revise." I allowed another twenty seconds of silence before urging kids, "Turn and share with your partner the words you'd add to this chapter."

As children talked, I listened in. Then, as if these revisions came from them, I displayed a "new beginning," written on a Post-it and placed carefully on the original draft:

> Imagine the accidents that can happen on the playground. A kid slips off the monkey bars. Someone falls from the swings. A fifth-grader crashes into a little kid. Imagine the blood. Imagine the sprained ankle. When accidents happen, how should a kid get help?

I also added the answer to a question:

> Where is the first aid kit? The nurse keeps her first aid kit in a little suitcase, high up in a cupboard.

ACTIVE ENGAGEMENT

Challenge students to reread their writing, asking themselves "What decisions can I make as the boss of my own book?"

"Writers, look over the charts in this room," I pointed to them, "and consider the strategies you learned earlier this year. Then decide on your own which ones you want to use. Quickly look at the chapter or two that you've written and figure out what work you need to do. Jot assignments to yourself on a Post-it."

After two minutes, I recalled children's attention. "Give me a thumbs up if you jotted that you would create great beginnings." I looked around expectantly. "Thumbs up if you decided you wouldn't just fix the chapter beginnings but also whenever you started a subtopic *inside* a chapter." I paused again, waiting for this suggestion to sink in. "Thumbs up if you decided you'd ask and answer 'Who, What, Where, Why' questions. I see some of you have jotted that you will add specific information—colors, quotes, numbers.

You may not really be timing them. This glancing at your wristwatch gives you the chance to break eye-contact and appear busy elsewhere—a nonverbal cue that you're expecting them to get started without your help.

You can have these written before the minilesson on Post-its and the kids won't really glean that the ideas weren't harvested from them. What you will want to do, however, is to listen to their suggestions and address any misconceptions.

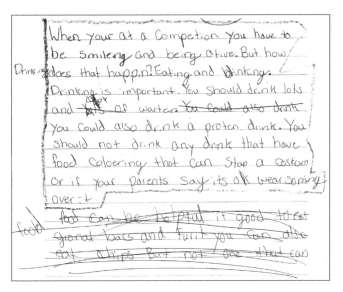

FIG. 11–1   Grace decides to keep some paragraphs and remove others.

"Remember that writers don't just decide *what* they will do, but also *where* they will do it. Now open up the chapter or chapter-parts you have so far. When you find the exact spot where you might make a revision, would you put a little star as a reminder?"

LINK

Remind students to create their own plans for revision.

"Writers, my point is that to be good at writing, you've got to make your own plans as a writer, you've got to form your own to-do lists, start your own writing for the parts that need fixing. Because it's *your* writing. No one else's.

"If you decide you need Post-its or tape to add flaps to your writing, you're the boss. Make that decision. There's the writing center with the supplies," I pointed. "Get working; you don't need my or anyone's permission to make your writing the best it can be.

"If later today you decide that you've finished a chapter and want to start a new one, you're the boss. Make that decision. Get more paper. Don't wait for permission or approval. Be the boss."

The Language You Use Matters

Give Kids a Sense of Agency, While Also Channeling Them to Revise

TODAY'S MINILESSON emphasized agency and revision—two things that don't go together often enough. You told the kids, "You are the boss of your writing," but what you really meant is, "You are the boss of your revisions." You'll want to be careful to support that message as you confer and lead small groups today. That doesn't mean, however, that you need to lower your standards and let kids get away with less than their best. Instead, you can use your language to convey that kids are in charge of their writing, yes, but also that you fully expect they'll find lots of ways to make their writing better and better.

Note the power of your language choices. Instead of saying, "Will you revise your beginnings?" you can ask, "Have you yet had a chance to work on making your beginnings even more special?" If the child says no, you might say, "Are you saving that for next? I do that too. Beginnings are so important that I sometimes save them until I am really in the swing of writing."

If a youngster seemed uncertain about how to revise, you could press, saying, "What were you thinking you *might* do to revise this part?" If the child signals that after a small tweak, she has decided she is (prematurely) done, saying, "It's good," you could reply, "Absolutely. Don't you love taking a page that is one of your best and making it even *better*? That is such a cool thing to do because your writing goes from good to truly great. Would it help if we both talked about *possible* ways that you *could* make this page even better?" Another line that often works is, "If you *were* going to make this even better, what *might* you do?" You could ask for more details, "How would that go, exactly?" And then, once the better version has been produced, "Yes, you are so right. That is so much better! Get it down on the page quickly before you forget it."

There will be some kids who are truly resistant to revising their writing, and that might be okay with you. "No problem," you might say. "Let me get you a fresh page so you can start your next chapter in your book. How will it go?" Once children realize the alternative to revision is drafting a whole new chapter, their resistance to revision may decrease.

> Do you know what kids love to play with? It ryhmes with boy and joy. It toys! Toys have different features. some make you feel cool, and feel not that lonely.

FIG. 11–2   Yadira revises her lead.

"Writers, I've seen you rereading your drafts and thinking about how you can add on to them—and you have added by thinking of questions readers might ask, by writing in specific details like names, numbers, colors. Today I want to remind you that writers don't just add; writers also *subtract*. Oftentimes, when I reread my information writing, I'll see that in a part of my writing, I talk all about something, and then I'll see a random bit of other information stuck into the paragraph—information that doesn't belong there. When I see that, I usually take out that off-topic info. It's kind of like sorting the laundry—if you found a sock in the T-shirt drawer, you would take it out, right? Information writers do the same thing.

"Let's practice this now. Will you and your partner go to a chapter in one of your books, and will you first remind yourself of what the chapter is all about? Juan's piece is all about candy. This chapter is about chocolate. So now, he is going to reread and see if there are things in his chapter that don't go with that topic. If so, he'll subtract those parts. He'll take them out." I added to our chart.

Celebrating Writers' Growing Independence

Congratulate writers on the independence they've increasingly shown. Ask partners to share with each other a recent example of smart, independent decision making.

"Today I want to celebrate something bigger than your writing—your independence. On July 4th in this country, we shoot fireworks to celebrate Independence Day, when the American colonies became independent from Great Britain, back in 1776. I'd love for today to be another Independence Day—for writers.

"Today, I felt that you were closer to becoming independent writers than you've ever been. You found problems in your writing, and you invented ways to solve those problems. Wow! You're growing up as writers.

"Will you think of an example of a problem in your writing that you found and fixed without needing to come to me?" I gave kids a moment to locate that spot in their drafts. "Turn and tell your partner."

WORKING WITH ENL STUDENTS

This session is already very supportive for ENLs:

◆ In the teaching section, you model how to make decisions for revision, referring to a step-by-step class chart.

To provide additional support for ENLs you might:

◆ Provide a smaller version of the "How to Write a Nonfiction Chapter Book" chart for students to refer to as they continue to make plans for their own writing.

◆ Ask students to cut apart the "Draft and Revise" anchor chart and tape bullet points from the anchor chart next to the places in their writing where they might revise in that way. This provides a clear visual for writers.

FIG. 11–3   Stella knows her cats! To read more chapters from her book, see Figure 10–2.

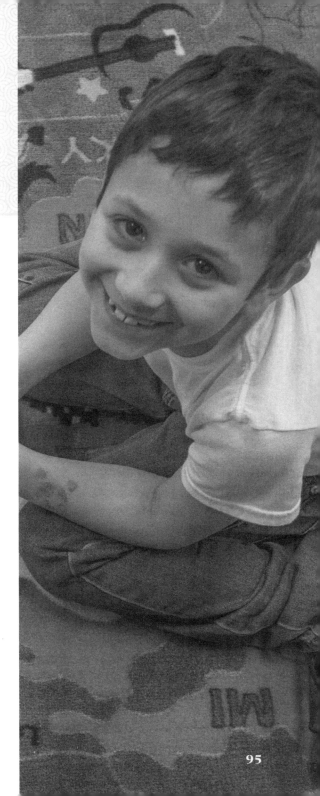

Designing Your Pages

IN THIS SESSION

TODAY YOU'LL teach students that nonfiction writers deliberately choose words and page design to match what they want to teach.

TODAY STUDENTS will draft a new chapter. Each student will choose a page design for the chapter that matches the content that she wants to write in that chapter. By the end of the session, each student will also have added a diagram to her book.

GETTING READY

✔ Choose a nonfiction book from your classroom library to show pages with text boxes, illustrations, and headings (see Connection).

✔ Display a variety of page designs to explain how each type suits different content (see Teaching).

✔ Display and add to "How to Write a Nonfiction Chapter Book" anchor chart (see Link).

✔ Gather some information books to show different formats and genres a writer can use to present content (see Conferring and Small-Group Work).

✔ Today's minilesson video:

hein.pub/UTLINFO_12

95

Designing Your Pages

CONNECTION

Acknowledge that up to this point, students have taught information with words. Explain that nonfiction writers teach not only through their words, but also through their page design.

"Writers, you have been doing such powerful work. How many of you have one chapter drafted and revised?" Kids signaled with thumbs up. "Fabulous. How many have two chapters?" Again, kids signaled. "You have written *a lot* of words. And that's my point: so far, all your teaching has been through words. That's a good place to start, but it is just a start."

I held up a nonfiction book from the classroom library and opened to a page with text boxes, an illustration, and headings. "The professional nonfiction writers we know and love, like Seymour Simon and Bobbie Kalman and Melissa Stewart, don't just teach with words. They also rely on the design of their pages to help them teach their readers. Listen up."

❖ **Name the teaching point.**

"Today I want to teach you that nonfiction writers choose the design and layout of their pages—the plan for where the illustration and the text boxes go—just as deliberately as they choose their words. They design the layout of their pages based on the effect they want to create."

TEACHING

Ask students to call to mind the next chapter they will draft.

"I want to help you make deliberate choices about the layout, the paper design, for the next chapter or two that you'll write today. Before we get started, will you think about what one of your next chapters will be about? Look at your table of contents if you need to." I gave students about fifteen seconds.

"I think my next chapter will be 'Fixing Injuries.' What are you thinking for your writing? Tell your partner what your next chapter will be." The children talked quickly, and then I pressed on.

This minilesson aims in part to build up your students' professional identities as writers. You are trying to help them feel that the book they are writing is for real, not just a class assignment. It is fun to think about the layout of a page. Tap their engagement and channel it toward more writing, This is a minilesson that sets them up to spend five minutes on paper choice and then forty minutes writing up a storm.

Note that in the last session as well, you gave kids a bit of time to settle on a topic they'd be writing about that day. Kids can listen to a minilesson best if they are applying it to a specific writing plan. For today, you will want kids to leave behind unfinished chapters and to tackle a brand-new chapter so that choosing paper is part of preparing to write.

Give an overview of popular page layouts, explaining why a writer would select each option. Channel kids to reflect on which layout matches their purpose in the upcoming chapter.

"Let's overview the most popular page designs, and decide why a writer would pick each of these. As I introduce each, will you think: 'Which one is a good fit for the chapter I'm about to write today?'

"Ready for the first paper design?" I revealed the "Picture This" kind of paper. "You see that the first thing a reader 'reads' is the picture, so this paper hooks readers and helps them imagine the whole topic right at the start. The paper says to readers, 'Picture this. Come into this world.' If you want readers to feel as if they are right there, looking at something, you might choose this paper.

"The second paper design, the 'Let Me Explain' paper, lets you explain with words and then add a diagram or chart or another kind of visual to remind readers of the key things you just said or to help with your explaining.

"Ready for page design number three? I call this 'Kinds, Parts, or Steps' paper design. What would you use this paper for? Turn and talk."

Nodding, I convened the kids. "Yes, you'd use it if you want to help readers understand all the different *kinds* of your topic—the kinds of dogs, the kinds of broken bones. Or you'd use it if you want to help readers understand the *steps* to your topic—the steps to beat your buddy in a video game or to put a cast onto a broken bone."

ACTIVE ENGAGEMENT

Ask the class to help choose one of the three page designs for a chapter in the class book. Use this as a way to promote that paper design.

"Are you thinking about the paper design to use for your next chapter? I've been thinking about what we should use for the next chapter in our class book. Let's decide together on the page design for 'Fixing Injuries.' Can I tell you how I was thinking that chapter might go, and then maybe you and your partner could make a suggestion?

"This chapter could talk about the things people do to fix injuries, like applying bandages to cuts and scraped knees, using stitches to close up a really bad wound, and making casts for when people break a bone. Which paper do you think would work best? Turn and talk."

A few seconds later I said, "I heard some good ideas. On the 'Kinds, Parts, or Steps' paper, we could make sketches of each way to treat injuries and then write about each of them. You guys are good at this."

Channel the class to help a student who is apt to use a different paper design option—just to promote a second design.

"Aiden thinks his chapter on 'Dog Shelters' might start by giving readers a feel for what it is like to walk into a shelter and see crates of dogs everywhere. Which design do you think might work for him and why? Turn and talk."

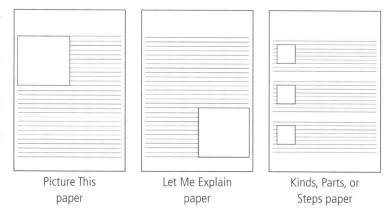

Picture This
paper

Let Me Explain
paper

Kinds, Parts, or
Steps paper

Teachers, if kids are writing on notebook paper, you can show them how they can tape large labels onto that paper to give the notebook paper a layout that resembles these.

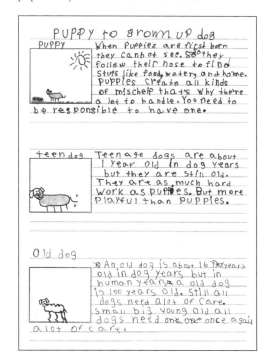

FIG. 12–1 Maria matches her content to the page designs.

The class agreed that Aiden might open his page with a picture that captured the chaos of the shelter, and then some words that describe it as well. After that he could tell more facts about the shelter. Students suggested that he use the "Picture This" paper design.

Debrief in ways that highlight the replicable work that you hope all your writers have learned to do.

"Writers, as you think about the paper design that might match your plans for your chapter, that leads you to think, 'How might the chapter go?' When you get ideas for your chapter, remember that it can help to write a few words along the margin as reminders about the subtopics you might talk about. Those words along the margin almost become an abbreviated table of contents for the chapter."

LINK

Ask partners to discuss what work on the anchor chart they will do today. Make suggestions phrased as questions and send kids off to do the work they've selected to do.

"Writers, think what you will do today. You'll be choosing one of the paper designs for your next chapter, but my hunch is that actually you will be doing all the things on our anchor chart to plan, rehearse, and draft another chapter. Will you review our chart to remind yourself of the work you need to do today? I've inserted today's teaching point into it. Tell your partner which of these things you'll do today."

The children talked, and I stepped in to voice over, "How many of you are actually finishing a chapter before doing anything else?" Some kids indicated that was their plan, and I sent them off. "How many of you will be sketching/drawing first—either for 'Picture This' paper, or for 'Kinds, Parts, or Steps' paper?" Many kids said that was their first step, and again I waved them off.

One writer asked what to do if she had four kinds, not three. I asked the kids that remained on the rug, "Writers, one of you just asked an important question. She asked, 'I want to use the "Kinds, Parts, or Steps" paper. But my chapter needs *four* boxes, not three. What should I do?'"

"What do you think I suggested?" After thirty seconds, I called out. "If you said I told this writer she could make new paper, you're right! If you don't find the paper design you need, make your *own* paper design. You'll find supplies at the writing center: blank sheets, rulers, markers, and lined sections to glue in. All of you—get going."

Quick, In-the-Moment Assessment and Response

Y OU WILL WANT to do some lightning-fast assessments today to see what your youngsters are doing.

If . . .	Then, this is what you might do . . .
A writer has a TOC, but the actual chapters don't match that TOC.	This happens to most writers. Once a writer starts writing, the text itself leads him to have new ideas. Remind this writer to revise the TOC.
Writing within a chapter is not structured or organized.	You might gather a small group and say, "Pull your table of contents page from your writing folder and compare the organization of your book with your TOC." Then say, "You may notice that your table of contents is like a 'to-teach' list for your book, with different categories of information that you want to teach your reader. You can practice this same work making to-teach lists for your chapters." I handed out Post-its and said, "Make a quick to-teach list for the chapter you are writing now. You might ask yourself, 'What would my reader expect to learn in a chapter titled _____?' Try this now and then use your lists to make sure your chapter is organized in a way that will make sense to your readers."

If . . .	Then, this is what you might do . . .
The chapters seem to overlap or repeat information.	Teach this writer to subtract information that repeats or overlaps. Then perhaps help the writer imagine some entirely different chapters. One way to do that is to think of those new chapters written in other formats or even other genres. What about a how-to chapter? A Q&A (question and answer) chapter? A chapter that is one long story, related to the topic? You might pull out an information book and use its contents to help jog this writer to imagine possibilities. The writer could also start a whole new book on a new topic.
If a writer has not elaborated within the chapter	Remind the writer to add on, to say more. You've taught that in this unit, as well as in the earlier narrative unit, when kids learned to write with twin sentences and to write things bit by bit, moving through a terrain in small steps, not big ones. Coach this writer to write with specific and particular details, and concrete information: numbers, names, quotes, descriptions, facts.

If . . .	Then, this is what you might do . . .
Writers are having trouble keeping up a steady volume of writing.	Look around your room and research the reasons. How many kids seem to be lingering behind the daily expectation of one to two pages a day? Is it a few kids or more than half the class? If it is half your class, then critically examine what happens during "writing time." Are your minilessons going overtime and eating into children's independent writing? Does the room become too noisy for writers to concentrate? Is there actually an *expectation* that children will write independently for an extended uninterrupted period of time? If you have been unclear, set the expectation now, and demand both quality *and* volume.

"Writers, most of the pages you have chosen include a spot for illustrations. I'll give you two tips about illustrations. First, any illustration will be more helpful to readers if it has a caption underneath that explains what is going on. Sometimes the caption explains how the illustration goes with the writing. Labels arrowed into an illustration may also help.

"The other tip is that your illustrations do not need to be drawings or photos. You've probably seen books with diagrams, right? Diagrams usually show how something works or how to do something. They often have arrows or numbers to show that things go from this, to this, to that. Work with your partner and for just for a second,

make a quick diagram to show how you do something that one of you is writing about in your book: how you make a skateboarding jump or how you comb your cat. Help each other. You have three minutes to work."

The kids worked. Then I said, "Before you finish up, take one second to leave yourself some notes if you find a place to add a diagram into your writing. You could make the diagram at home tonight, or take a quick moment tomorrow to make a diagram. You can make the diagram on a Post-it if you don't have space, and you can figure out later how to get it into the text."

Gallery Walk

Celebrate today's work by having students conduct a silent gallery walk of work from today.

"Writers, let's end class by studying work you have just done. Place the chapter you drafted today at your workspace, and take a moment to admire it with a stranger's eyes. What did you do well that you'd like others to notice? Mark that spot with a Post-it. You might even draw an arrow or a star.

"Now walk around the room silently, admiring the work of your classmates. You might even notice something another writer in the class has done that you might want to try!"

WORKING WITH ENL STUDENTS

This session is already very supportive for ENLs:

◆ The session builds learners' identities so they think of themselves as writers.

◆ Students get multiple opportunities for low-stress oral rehearsal with partners.

◆ Students can use drawing, diagramming, and design skills to create or revise their chapters.

To provide additional support for ENLs, you might:

◆ Use examples from mentor texts that students know well so the new concept is embedded in familiar texts.

◆ Give examples of how each kind of paper might be used to give students a vision of what their book could look like.

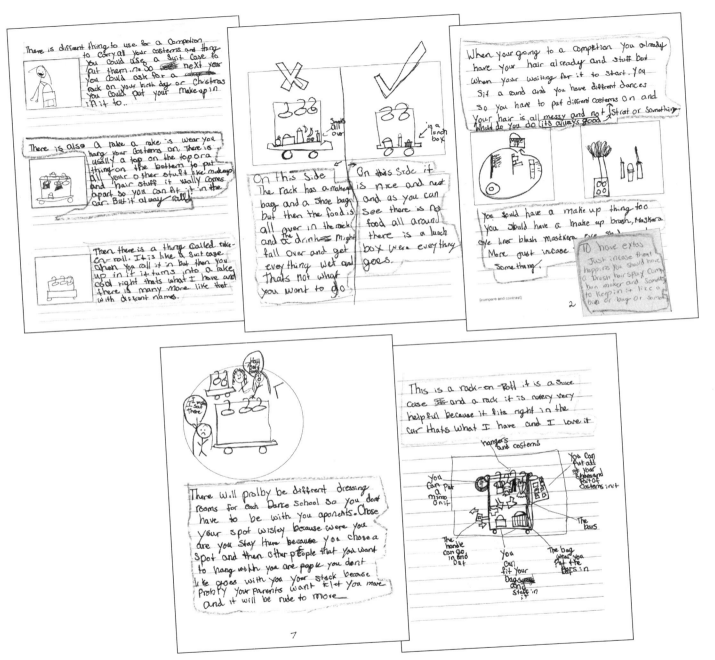

FIG. 12–2 This gallery walk shows how Grace has used a variety of page designs to match the content of her chapters in her book *Dance Competition*.

Editing for Paragraphs

IN THIS SESSION

TODAY YOU'LL teach students that information writers edit their writing for clear paragraphs before they send this writing out into the world.

TODAY STUDENTS will reread and edit their chapters, using the editing checklist. They will edit for *all* of the items on the checklist, including making sure that sentences inside a paragraph all fit together. Some students may also need to draft another chapter. Today is the last day to work on this book. They will recopy one fully edited chapter for tomorrow's celebration.

GETTING READY

- Display "Staying Safe" chapters from the class book (see Teaching and Active Engagement).
- Display "The New and Improved Editing Checklist" (see Link).
- Provide revision tools (scissors, paper strips, Post-its, tape) (see Link, Conferring and Small-Group Work, Mid-Workshop Teaching, Share).

- Give each student sheets of writing paper to write clean drafts for homework (see Share).

- Today's minilesson video:
  hein.pub/UTLINFO_13

Editing for Paragraphs

CONNECTION

Announce that this is the last day for students to work on their chapter books before they are published. Remind children of all they know to edit their writing so it is the best it can be.

"Writers, your chapters are filling up. Most of you are almost done with your books—am I right?" I nodded along with them. "Tomorrow we'll celebrate all your hard work on your chapter books. Let's take time today to think about that part of the writing process that every writer turns to when it's almost time to send a manuscript out into the world. Remember we talked earlier about how I try to make myself presentable before I come to school? I brush my hair, wash up. And remember that we talked about how our writing, too, needs to be spiffed up before it goes out into the world?

"You already know a lot about editing. List across your fingers five things that you check for when you reread your writing one last time before deciding it's presentable." I let the kids list across their fingers, and then joined them to make a shared editing list. "You are right to check for end punctuation, capitalization, spelling, and run-ons, and to make sure others can read your writing. Today, I have the chance to add one more item to that list, and I've been thinking and thinking about what to add."

❖ **Name the teaching point.**

"Today, I want to teach you that information writers pay special attention to one thing when they edit. Above all, information writers think about their *paragraphs*. They make sure that every sentence inside a paragraph fits together."

TEACHING

Contextualize the point on paragraphs by suggesting that organization is a priority for information writers. Recruit students to help you reread a chapter in the class book, examining paragraphs.

"You might think, 'Huh? Why are paragraphs such a big deal?' If you think back over this unit, you'll realize that the one thing I have tried to teach is that information writers *organize*. Information writers *sort the laundry*. They develop tables of contents for their books *and* for their chapters. Those tables of contents help to group—to chunk—similar

◆ COACHING

Paragraphing is a really big deal because it reinforces text structure both for readers and writers. Once students learn that a shift in subtopic should signal a new paragraph, they'll soon realize their writing consists of tons of tiny paragraphs—and that realization can lead writers to see the need for elaboration. The important thing is not that students paragraph this particular chapter book correctly but that they begin to get paragraphing into their bones.

information together. To sort the socks in one pile, the T-shirts in another. Paragraphs act like containers. They show readers that your information has been sorted and organized.

"Look at this start of the last chapter in our Kid Injuries book." I placed the "Staying Safe in the Car" chapter draft under the document camera.

"Looking at this draft, you might think: 'Beautiful paragraphing!' But don't be impressed too soon. Look carefully." I zoomed in on the starting sentences of the first paragraph. I read the paragraph aloud, then looked up. "Huh! We just were jerked from seatbelts to sleepy driving—and from riding in a car to driving a car. Listen again. See if you can hear that there are two subtopics in this one paragraph."

I reread, my voice accentuating the disconnect. "Thumbs up if you sense that this should be divided into two parts, two paragraphs." Turn and tell your partner where you'd break this." As children talked, I placed a pilcrow (paragraph mark—¶) conspicuously before the words, "It is dangerous to drive . . ."

Debrief what you just did so students can replicate this in their own writing.

"Did you see that mark I just made to split this paragraph? See how splitting this made the organization of our chapter so much better? Information writers reread their writing, paragraph by paragraph, asking 'Is there an organizational problem here? Does it look like I've stuffed socks in with T-shirts?' And they fix mess-ups by giving each subtopic its own paragraph, with white space around it."

ACTIVE ENGAGEMENT

Set students up to read the next paragraph to see if splitting it into two will improve its organization.

"Right now, let's read this next paragraph together. Will you hold up a hand and call 'Stop!' when you think we might be starting on a *new* subtopic?"

I motioned for children to read "Staying Safe at Home" aloud with me. Sure enough, most kids noted the break when the passage switched from talking about safety in bedrooms to safety in kitchens. We marked the spot with a pilcrow. I asked, "Why should a new paragraph begin here? Turn and tell your partner."

"Writers, it looked like this page was beautifully paragraphed when we started. But reading closely made it clear that we had some work to do—and I am pretty sure that is true for your chapters as well."

Staying Safe in the Car

One way to stay safe while you are riding in a car is to buckle your seat belt. "I've never had to remove a dead person from a seat belt," one traffic police officer said. He meant that if someone is buckled into a seat belt, that person will probably survive even dangerous accidents. It is dangerous to drive long distances on the highway if you are short on sleep. Take a break and stretch your legs or ask someone else to drive for a while.

Staying Safe at Home

Your bedroom may have clutter on the floor. You and other people might trip over that clutter. Also, don't let wires criss cross the room because again, they can make you and other people trip. Your kitchen is another place to watch for safety. Don't place knives where toddlers can reach them.

LINK

Send children off to write and channel them to make their writing presentable for tomorrow's celebration, reminding them of the teaching of the day.

"When you write today, will you work to make your writing presentable before tomorrow's celebration? You will find and fix run-on sentences, capitalize first letters of names and places, fix your spelling . . .

"But don't *just* work with a pen—you may need a pair of *scissors*. I've left some on each table. Cut out the smaller paragraphs that are hiding in the big chunks of your writing and separate them so your reader can see them. Remember to give each subtopic a paragraph of its own. A reader's eye *needs* white space, so see if you can create white space around your most beautiful paragraphs to make the organization of your ideas visible to the world."

I updated the editing checklist.

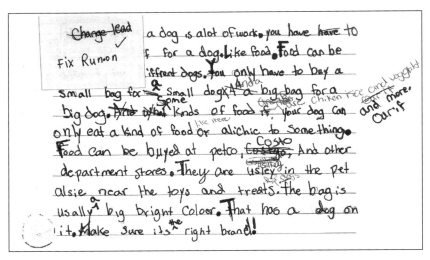

FIG. 13–1   This writer uses all she knows about editing.

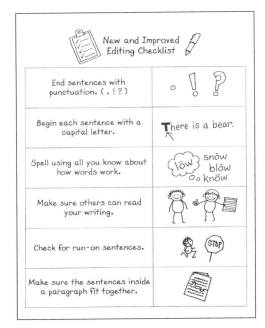

Supporting Spelling and Conventions Work

Coach children at every opportunity in conferences and small groups to carry and transfer previous teaching:

Run-on sentences

- "Look through each paragraph. Count the number of ending punctuation marks. Just *one*? In *seven lines of text*? Give the reader's eye a break! Look for run-on sentences and fix them."

- "Take out the Scotch-tape words that make your sentences run on and on. Can you replace words like *and*, *but*, *so*, or *then* with a period? Go for it!"

Paragraphing

- "How many paragraphs have you made on each page? That *entire* page is a *single* paragraph? Check sentence by sentence! I *bet* you teach more than one thing in there! Where can you insert the pilcrow?"

- "You know that in information texts, a paragraph teaches *one* thing. Move through your writing with the eyes of a stranger, looking at each paragraph. Can you find the *one* thing that each paragraph teaches? If there are two things in there, split that up into two paragraphs."

Capitalization

- "Ask, 'Is it the name of a place, a person, or a month?' If so, capitalize it."

- "Ask, 'Is this the start of a new sentence?' If so, capitalize it."

- "Look down the page. Where else do you have a name of a place or person? Flip the page and look through *all* your chapters for places to add a capital letter."

Spelling

- "Say the word slowly. Ask, 'What sounds do I hear? Write those sounds.'"

- "Ask, 'Does it look right?' If not, try it a few different ways in the margin."

- "Tap out the syllables. You need at least one vowel for each syllable."

MID-WORKSHOP TEACHING **Editing for Paragraphs Reopens the Door to Revision**

"Writers, I see many of you cutting apart your writing into paragraphs, adding white space that brings out the structure of your writing. Wow! The organization of your writing is beginning to look so clear. I'm also noticing, though, that cutting your writing into paragraphs means that where there once was a big chunk of writing, now you have several tiny-looking paragraphs. Thumbs up if this is true." Half a dozen students gave me a thumbs up.

"If this is the case, if your newborn paragraphs look especially skimpy, don't hesitate to do a quick revise." I pointed to the anchor chart. "You can use all you know about information writing to elaborate, to add on. You can ask a 'Who, What, Where, Why' question about the information in your tiny paragraph and answer that question. You can work to make the beginning of this paragraph special: ask a question, paint a picture with words. You can write with specific details, quotes, colors, numbers. Use all that you know to quickly revise these newborn paragraphs so they have enough meat on them.

"Remember, though—a tiny paragraph about one thing is *much* better than an endless paragraph that covers a mixture of things. So get those scissors and snip, snip, organize!"

Choosing and Perfecting One Chapter for Tomorrow's Celebration

Announce that tomorrow, the class will celebrate the work of this bend, and set kids up to select a favorite chapter to edit and perfect now, and then copy onto clean paper tonight.

"Writers, tomorrow we'll celebrate the accomplishment of writing these books. So you have between now and tomorrow to get them ready for celebration. Then we have one more bend in this unit, and in that bend, you'll be going back to one of the books you wrote at the very start of this unit, and making that book *worlds* better.

"But for now, the job is to get ready to put these books behind you. Between today and tomorrow, you won't have time to edit and recopy every single page of these books. We could do that—we could take the next few days and just work on perfecting and recopying, but I think your time is better used taking one more book from so-so to great.

"So I'm going to suggest you just edit and perfect one chapter for now—and that will be the one chapter you celebrate tomorrow. Your first job is to choose your best chapter, to reread it with a stranger's eyes, noticing any little details that need repair. Do you have periods there so you don't have run-on sentences? Did you spell as best you can (and spell your word wall words correctly)? When someone reads this chapter over, will it make sense? Above all, did you write with white spaces between paragraphs?

"Instead of talking with a partner, use your share time to prepare for your writing homework for tonight. I'll give each of you a nice clean page or two on which to recopy your chapter (after you have corrected it) and you'll make a whole new, almost perfect draft of that chapter. Your job will be to get this one chapter to be the neatest, cleanest, easiest-to-read chapter possible.

"Get to work!"

HOW TO WRITE A NONFICTION CHAPTER BOOK...
- THINK of a topic
- ORGANIZE your information
  - make a Table of Contents
- PLAN your chapter before you write it
  - jot keywords or quick sketches
  - think of the Table of Contents for the chapter
  - ask "What will interest my reader?"
- DRAFT and REVISE
  - think of the questions people will ask (who? what? where? when? why? how?) and answer them
  - write with specific details: names, numbers, colors, sizes, shapes
  - make your beginning special
  - be the boss of your own writing star places that need revision
  - don't just add... subtract parts too!
- EDIT
  - make sure every sentence in the paragraph fits together

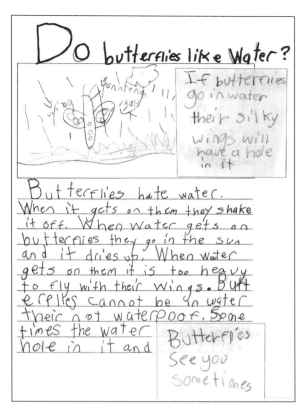

FIG. 13–2   Jahmiya is proudest of her chapter on why butterflies hate water.

FIG. 13–3   Michael takes help from a peer to double-check his edits.

WORKING WITH ENL STUDENTS

This session is already very supportive for ENLs:

◆ There are multiple opportunities to practice paragraphing in the minilesson.

◆ The conferring and small-group work sections provide opportunities for you to reinforce earlier teaching and support students in working on run-on sentences, paragraphing, capitalization, and spelling.

To provide additional support for ENLs you might:

◆ Provide a quick additional active engagement, with another easy run-on paragraph or two so that students are given additional practice splitting paragraphs.

Celebrating Growth by Giving Feedback

IN THIS SESSION

TODAY YOU'LL teach students that writers help each other by giving powerful feedback in the form of specific, detailed compliments.

TODAY STUDENTS will celebrate the information chapter books they have written. In partnerships, they will read each other's writing and give each other specific compliments.

GETTING READY

✔ Prepare a list of student pairs who will work together today. You will display this list in class (see Teaching and Active Engagement, Link, and Share).

✔ Make sure students have their clean drafts from last night's homework (see Connection).

✔ Put pink Post-its on students' tables (see Connection).

✔ Display "Complimenting Each Other's Writing" chart (see Teaching and Active Engagement).

✔ Display "Time to Eat!" article (see Teaching and Active Engagement).

✔ Today's minilesson video:

hein.pub/UTLINFO_14

Celebrating Growth by Giving Feedback

CONNECTION

Ask writers to set out their fixed-up chapter on their desks before gathering in the meeting area.

"Writers, before you come to the meeting area, will you find a way to put your one cleaned-up, fixed-up chapter into its proper place in your book? You can staple or tape or use paper clips, or just slide it into position for now.

"Then will you set up your workspace so it's ready for a celebration of your work? Put a Post-it on your very best chapter (I've left pink Post-its at your tables). If there are other parts of your book that you especially like (and there probably are), put pink Post-its on those parts as well.

"In a minute, one of your classmates will study your writing."

Set students up to give each other feedback on their writing. Emphasize the value of specific positive feedback. Encourage writers to talk about what works in each other's writing.

"Today, as we get ready to celebrate your work from this bend, I want to help you become better cheerleaders of each other. I want to give you tips about feedback that *teachers* tend to know, that kids are usually not told."

❖ **Name the teaching point.**

"Here is the tip I want to teach you. A compliment works best and means the most if it is very specific. So if you want to give super-powerful feedback, you need to find something specific, something detailed, that the writer has done and put that thing into words."

TEACHING AND ACTIVE ENGAGEMENT

Explain a process for finding some aspect of the writing to compliment and for giving feedback.

"In a bit, I'm going to ask you to partner with another writer—just for today—to give each other compliments." I displayed a list of the pairings I'd chosen. "Before you do that, I want to teach you how to find something to compliment in a classmate's writing."

◆ COACHING

Today's session is unusual, so you we suggest you scan the entire plan for the day before embarking on it.

The secret behind color-coding the Post-its pink is to help distinguish them from other Post-its in the room. Your notes could be a different color.

We're suggesting that you pair writers so that this doesn't become a popularity contest, which of course can leave some kids feeling blue. If you aren't worrying about that with your particular class, it would be terrific to just ask kids to move from one writer to the next in an organic fashion.

"First, pick up your partner's writing and read it to yourself like it is gold, like it's worth a million dollars. Your job is to be blown away by the most beautiful, most powerful, most honest, most surprising parts.

"Then as you read the piece like it's gold, let a part of the writing make you think, or feel, or notice . . . and when that happens, pause. Try to put into words why that part got through to you. That's hard. It can help to see if the writer did that same thing in other places too."

Take writers through the steps of the process as a class, using another writer's piece. First read the piece together like it is gold, looking for a part that stands out and moves you in some way.

"You ready to practice getting good at supporting each other? Remember the steps you'll take." I displayed the "Complimenting Each Other's Writing" chart.

"Let's do this with my neighbor Otis's writing. Here's one chapter from his book about taking care of a little kid." I placed it on the document camera. "Let's do the first step and read this like it's gold. Read it aloud with me. Ready?"

> ## Time to Eat!
>
> When you are helping take care of a little kid, you might have to help feed that kid. It's important to make sure the little kid is in a high chair and buckled in. Then you need some food in a bowl and a spoon. It's also a good idea to make sure the little kid wears a bib. Now you are ready! Put some food on the spoon and feed it to the little kid.
>
> My first advice is BE CAREFUL! Sometimes little kids spit their food out. For example, I helped feed my little sister peas last week and she spit them out all over me. I had smushed peas on my face and on my shirt and even some in my hair. Gross! So, be careful and be ready to duck!

Point out that students noticed a part that stands out. Ask them to identify it and box it. Then push students to think about what the writer did that got to them, and to put that into words.

"Writers. I see a bunch of you laughing. You let a part of the writing get to you. That's step 2, right? Tell me, what part made you laugh?"

Some kids called out, "The part where Otis's sister spit peas out all over him!" and I boxed that section. Then I asked them to name what step came next and they chimed in, "Think, 'What did the writer do that got to me?'"

I gave them a tip. "Think about why you reacted to the part in a particular way—in this case with laughter." Then I said, "Give it a try, writers. Talk to the person next to you. Go!"

If you'll recall, Otis is the name of your (imaginary) neighborhood pal who has been seeking your advice about becoming a better, stronger writer. His writing threads through a number of the minilessons in this unit (and other units).

Listening in, I heard Edgar say, "He made it so funny."

"How?" I coached.

Edgar said, "It's funny how his sister spat peas on him!"

"He described something funny in a way that would make readers laugh," I rephrased in a way that was transferable to the writing process.

Gather writers back and have one pretend to be the writer of the piece while you model giving some feedback, writer to writer.

After a minute, I called the kids back. "Trying to name what a writer did to get readers to pause and react is tricky. You have to look beyond what the writing *says*—and think about how it *works*.

"Let's do the last step. Will one of you volunteer to be Otis? I'll model how I would give feedback, and then you can do it, too."

Once I had a volunteer in front of me, I directed the class to notice how I gave the child my full attention and how I talked to her, writer to writer. Looking the child right in the eye I said, "Otis, I was just reading the section of your article on feeding the baby. Can I give you some feedback?"

When my volunteer nodded, I said, "This section was so easy to learn from! The way you named it 'Time to Eat!' helped me know right from the start what this part was going to be about. *And* the beginning," I read the first sentence, "let me know *exactly* what you were going to teach me. The focus of this section was clear, so it was easy to learn from."

Give writers a chance to practice giving feedback. Have one student play the role of the writer of the piece the class is studying and one give feedback.

"Writers, I want you to try this now. Partner 1, you be Otis. Partner 2, you give feedback. Tell Otis the specific part you like and what Otis did to make that part so good—to get you to pause, and react. Go!"

I gave kids a couple of minutes to do this, then said, "Otis is gonna feel great about his writing, hearing these specific compliments! I'll be sure to pass them on."

When you rephrase what a child says about the content of one piece so that it is a transferable craft move, you model the stance of "reading like a writer."

Here, I deliberately give feedback on something that most students probably won't notice on their own. I do this for two reasons. One, I am going to set up writers to give feedback on other aspects of the piece, and I don't want to take away the low-hanging fruit. Two, I am calling students' attention to something that I want to be sure they do in their own pieces and I know that focus is often a predictable problem. If your writers are more advanced and you think they will notice the clear focus of Otis's work, then you might model giving feedback on something more sophisticated—perhaps how he has varied his sentence structure, making it more engaging to read.

LINK

Set partners up to celebrate each other's writing by giving specific, detailed compliments.

"Writers, you've worked so hard on your chapter books. Pause and think about how much better your writing has become. We're going to spend the whole day thinking about that progress.

"Now go to the writer I've paired you with (I pointed to the pairing chart). The writer named first on this chart should look at the work of the writer named second. Start by reading the fixed-up chapter like it is gold. Remember, you are finding ways to celebrate that writing. Look at the 'Complimenting Each Other's Writing' chart so you have a process to follow. Look also at our anchor chart to remind yourself of things your writer may have done. You might even compare some of the writing your partner did in Bend I with his or her most recent writing. Above all, you'll tell your partner what he or she has done that you appreciate. Get started."

After a while, I channeled writers to switch roles.

FIG. 14–1   Pink Post-it compliments decorated everyone's chapters on this day.

Compliment Writers on Their Growth

TODAY, FLEX *YOUR* FEEDBACK MUSCLES, giving your students detailed compliments that acknowledge their growth as information writers. Before you say, "Off you go!" think about the people who have helped you become all you can be. Think of the people who've given you feedback that you still recall, years later. Chances are, those people saw more in you than you saw in yourself. Goethe once said, "Treat a person as he is, and he will remain as he is. Treat a person as he could be, and he will become all he could be."

Resolve to be fully present today. Respond to each child's work with awe at the power you see in that child. Take the advice that you gave your students. Don't approach a piece of writing thinking, "Is this any good?" Instead, approach the draft thinking, "This work is gold." Read the writing with reverence. Savor its cadence, the author's handprints in the syntax, the choice of words, the smudges of effort.

You might try some starter phrases, "You are the kind of writer who . . ." or "Not many kids . . . but you are able to . . ." Or try this. "See how much you have grown in the past two weeks? You used to . . . but now you . . . You're like a shooting star! Your writing started as this good," you say making a measuring gesture at a medium height, "now it's this good," gesturing much higher. "I can't wait to see this next week . . ."

Some writers' work may disappoint you, but you can still convey trust and belief. "I've seen your talent for writing. The way you . . . shows you've got a writer's heart. The way you . . . shows you've got a writer's eyes. So I always look forward to reading your writing . . . But there are a few parts of this book that look like you throw any ol' thing on the page. You are wasting your potential! You just have today and this evening, and then our last bend, to turn a corner as a writer. Start with this chapter. Make it *way* better, 'cause I know you can. Get to work."

One secret is to say a paragraph of support, not just a sentence. Be specific and personal. To a writer who has written more pages than ever, you might say, "I'm blown away by the writer you've become. The word *prolific* describes you—that means you write with tremendous volume. Remember always, you're a prolific writer who fills line after line, page after page."

To a writer who filled his book with facts about his topic, you could say, "I've been reading your book. My brain is exploding! This one page is chock full of information about food in Canada. You've taught me about eating out in Canada, grocery shopping, organic food. Like Seymour Simon, you pack your text full of information. Keep up the amazing teaching and writing."

In each example, you've gloried in your writers' growth. You might have done this by using a special term, like *prolific*, compared their work to that of a pro, or used a metaphor to name what's noteworthy.

Going forward, remember the power of positive feedback for your writers. When you give meaningful compliments, you're also modeling for kids how to give compliments to each other.

MID-WORKSHOP TEACHING **Noticing and Celebrating Growth in Your Own Writing**

"Writers, I want you to do something important. Will you sit alone beside your own writing?

"Now, *you* will be your own writing partner and *you* will read your own writing. Start with your writing from the start of the unit, then shift to the writing you've done more recently. Think about ways your writing has grown and about the most powerful, beautiful parts. Look at the chapter you chose to share—the pink Post-it chapter—but this time, look at your other chapters too. Read your writing the same way that you read a partner's piece. Think about what parts stand out and why you like them and push yourself to find words to describe what works in your writing."

Read Aloud Each Other's Writing Like It's Gold
A Celebration

Announce that the class will celebrate. Send several partnerships with their newly revised chapters to one of the four corners of the rug to read each other's writing like it's gold.

"Writers, in a minute we're going to celebrate. Will you and your one-day partner come to the rug and sit in a small group in one of the four corners of the rug?" Once kids had sat and I'd engineered them into roughly equal groups, I said, "These will be your celebration groups. Each of you will share the part you just admired from your partner's writing (not your own). You'll read aloud just a few lines or a paragraph, and you'll read it like it is gold. Then you can tell your group what you liked about that passage—and then, *each* of you will tell your partner what *you* like in that passage. Do this for each person in the group. You ready? This is going to take some really skilled complimenting!"

Debrief. Compliment children on their writing and hard work and encourage them to learn from their own and each other's growth.

"Writers, you've worked hard and it shows. Take the compliment you heard earlier to heart and keep it in mind as you move to new writing projects. I hope you feel proud!"

WORKING WITH ENL STUDENTS

This session is already very supportive for ENLs:

◆ The step-by-step chart, "Complimenting Each Other's Writing," is specific and easy to understand and use. It will help kids look closely at another writer's work and offer meaningful feedback.

To provide additional support for ENLs you might:

◆ Provide a few sentence starters to support speaking in the language of compliments—"I like the way you . . ." "I notice that you . . ." "This part of your writing makes me . . ."

◆ Fishbowl two writers giving compliments. Voice over what the partners are saying and doing to make the work replicable.

Bend III: Taking Your Writing from Good to Great

Bend III is an important and ambitious addition to this book. The youngsters are invited to select the book they care most about from Bend I, and to devote the final portion of the unit to revising that book. The invitation is a setup for youngsters to embrace revision, as the books they wrote at the start of the unit were written in a single day, and represented the work youngsters were able to do before they began on the journey of this unit. Their skills and ambitions are far grander now, so when they are asked to think about ways they can make that first book much, much better, devoting an entire week to that project, they're sure to have lots of ideas.

Your emphasis at the start of this bend is serious. You rally your kids to embrace goal-driven, "deliberate" practice. The first day of this bend debunks the myth of the 10,000 hours—the notion that people get better at something just by doing it, relentlessly. "You don't get benefits from mechanical repetition but by adjusting your execution over and over to get closer to your goal," says Anders Ericsson, the psychologist whose research sparked the myth in the first place. John Hattie's research firmly backs the critical need for deliberate practice, one where students—rather than teachers—set goals.

You fuel their aspirations for revision by reminding them that information writers often find that it helps to divide a text into subtopics, devoting either a chapter or a subsection to each subtopic. Your writers will probably label each page of their little three- or four-page booklets as a chapter, and your job will be to help them develop the contents of those pages.

You teach kids to do that by suggesting they study a mentor text that you provide. This is an article about bulldogs, and it uses subheadings rather than chapter titles to section off the subtopics. The text is a mosaic of specific concrete information, and you point out to your students that good information writing is that way. It is made from a variety of concrete information, cobbled together. The bulldog mentor text includes descriptions, statistics, quotes, and comparisons, and you encourage your students to bring equal variety into their writing. That point is made lightly, in the connection to the second session in this bend, and you may make the decision to expand on that connection, turning it into an entire minilesson.

Soon you are teaching children that they can also bring more concrete, specific information into their writing if they tap into the people around them as sources of information, interviewing each other about their topics, and surveying each other. Your mid-workshop teaching on that day reminds youngsters that they can also gather information from experts on a topic by researching in nonfiction books.

Once students have learned to include more information in their drafts, it is a natural next step to teach them that actually, good information writing consists of a balance between information and ideas. Writing that is "fact, fact, fact" is far from ideal! Your students will learn that facts need to bolstered by a writer's own insights, and they'll learn to capture and develop *ideas*. You'll find enormous power in this session, especially for your more proficient writers.

The instruction on writing with a variety of information and on using interviews, surveys, and research to gather more information, combined with the instruction on writing with ideas, adds up to an emphasis on elaboration. If the focus in Bend II was on writing well-organized texts, the focus now is on writing with increasing elaboration. Doing this poses new demands on students' abilities to write well-organized texts, and woven throughout this bend is an emphasis on organizing the subsections within a chapter.

Finally, you encourage your students to revise with an eye on craft learned from mentor texts. And of course, they will organize their pages, bringing all they know about paragraphing and dividing topics into subtopics from Bend II.

The flow of the bend is such that youngsters progress from writing with more information (and more varied information) to including ideas that help readers see the significance of that information. Then you remind youngsters that beauty matters, that writing well matters. You'll use powerful mentor texts to inspire and drive students to make their writing more beautiful. The larger goal is for your students to learn to write in ways that get their readers to care about their topic. All this should reap quick rewards in the form of writing that is more deliberate and developed, sentences that echo with greater verve and voice.

Broadway by Jenna. A Bend I book written in 2 days.

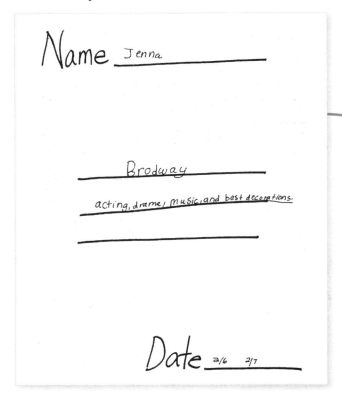

Name Jenna

Brodway

acting, drama, music, and best decorations.

Date 2/6 2/7

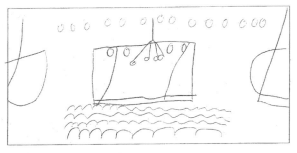

Brodway is humungus. Brodway has gold silver and diamond everyware. The out side has a humungus sighn of the shou ^(that is one) with glittery calerfull lights everyware ~~on~~ ^(around) the sighn. The halway is gold and silver and hage beatifull lights. Thats one reasen why it cost a lot of money to go ^(see a Brodway show.) ~~but~~ I'll tell you it's ^(definitly) worth it. Thats probily one reasen why its named best ^(one of the) theaters in the world!

Jenna teaches her reader about decorations on Broadway.

Broadway by Jenna. A completely
revised Bend III book written in 5 days.

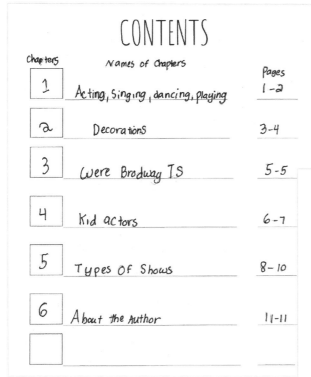

CONTENTS

Chapters

Names of Chapters   Pages

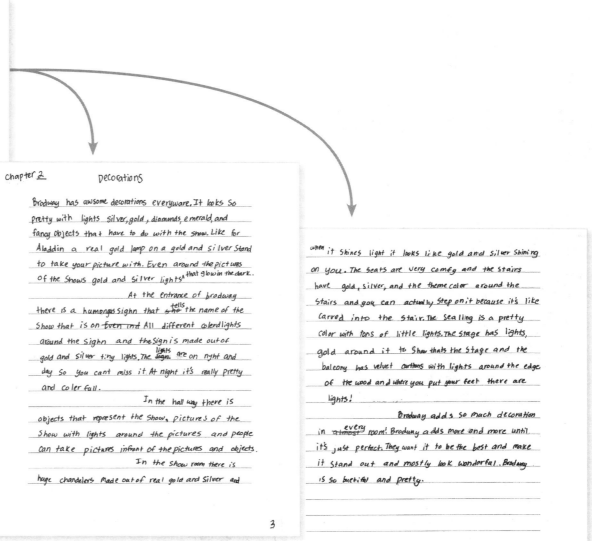

chapter 2   Decorations

Brodway has awsome decorations everyware. It looks So pretty with lights silver, gold, diamonds, emerald, and fancy objects that have to do with the show. Like for Aladdin a real gold lamp on a gold and silver Stand to take your picture with. Even around the pictures of the Shows gold and silver lights^that glow in the dark.

At the entrance of brodway there is a humongus sighn that tells the name of the Show that is on. Even and All different colerd lights around the sighn and the sign is made out of gold and Silver tiny lights. The lights are on nyht and day So you cant miss it. At night it's really pretty and coler full.

In the hall way there is objects that represent the Show, pictures of the Show with lights around the pictures and people can take pictures infront of the pictures and objects.

In the show room there is huge chandelers made out of real gold and Silver and

3

when it shines light it looks like gold and silver Shining on you. The seats are very comfy and the stairs have gold, silver, and the theme color around the stairs and you can actually Step on it because it's like Carved into the stair. The Sealing is a pretty color with tons of little lights. The stage has lights, gold around it to Show thats the stage and the balcony has velvet curtians with lights around the edge of the wood and where you put your feet there are lights!

Brodway adds so much decoration in every room! Broduny adds more and more until it's just perfect. They want it to be the best and make it stand out and mostly look wonderful. Brodway is so buetifl and pretty.

4

Jenna's revised chapter on decorations shows her
growth in both organization and elaboration.

Goal-Driven Deliberate Practice Matters

IN THIS SESSION

TODAY YOU'LL teach students that writers push themselves to grow by setting crystal clear goals and working deliberately to meet those goals.

TODAY STUDENTS will choose a book from Bend I that they will spend the week revising and expanding into a new chapter book. They will use a mentor text and writing checklist to set goals and begin revising their first book in dramatic ways.

GETTING READY

✔ Before this session, and throughout this bend, be sure that your writing center is stocked with writing and revision tools (paper choices, tape, paper strips, green Post-its, envelopes, scissors).

✔ Students bring the most interesting book they've written and a pen to the meeting area (see Connection).

✔ Distribute large green Post-its to each student to jot ideas for revision (see Connection).

✔ Display the anchor charts from Bends I and II (see Connection).

✔ Provide a copy of the "Bulldogs" mentor text and Information Writing Checklist to each student (see Teaching and Active Engagement).

✔ For small groups as needed, print out easier or more challenging versions of "Bulldogs" (see Conferring and Small-Group Work).

✔ Today's minilesson video:

hein.pub/UTLINFO_15

Studying Mentor Texts to Revise in Big Ways

CONNECTION

Rally writers toward the new bend in the unit by teaching them the basics of Hattie's research on the importance of goal-driven deliberate practice.

"Writers, before you come to the meeting area, will you look over the books you wrote at the start of this unit, and choose one that interests you the most? Choose quickly, bring a pen, and come join me." As the kids arrived in the meeting area, I gave each a small pile of big green Post-its.

Once the kids had convened, I said, "Look at the book you are holding and realize that is what your best information writing looked like two weeks ago. You have grown, right? Researchers have found that when you start learning to do something, people can get better quickly, which is what has happened to you, right? Your growth curve goes like this." I drew a diagram that showed a horizontal base, then a spurt of vertical growth.

"To show yourself and the world how much you have grown, you will have a chance to *revise* this book. You'll be able to work on this one book for the rest of our unit, and in the end you'll publish it. Right now, remember all that you've learned about information writing. Start using these green Post-its (green for growth!) to jot ideas you have for revising your book."

As kids worked, I skimmed the class book and added large green Post-its onto a few pages, doing so in ways that gave ideas to the students for ways they could revise their writing. I added two green Post-its to page 1. On one I wrote, "Make into a chapter." On the other I wrote, "Use different kinds of paper." Then I turned to page 2.

This portion of your minilesson will take longer than usual, but the good news is the time will be devoted to kids working, not to you talking. Don't, however, persist with this too long. The goal is not for kids to produce an all-encompassing list of to-dos—the goal is for them to get their minds going on ways they can engage in significant, large-scale revision.

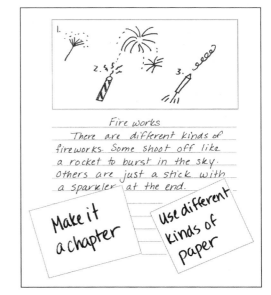

FIG. 15–1a   Page 1

I quickly added a jot—"Make it a chapter"—to the green Post-it on page 2, then turned to the next page that read:

> July 4th is famous for fireworks. The day is the United States' birth-day. Many people celebrate with a big fireworks celebration.

Finally on the green Post-it on page 3, I wrote, "Chapter on 4th of July?"

As kids worked, I coached. "You'll have a whole week to work on this, so my best guess is you'll turn your pages into chapters and sometimes you'll start over. You'll probably also make new pages—even a new chapter or two."

I also coached, "I love the way you are using our charts to remind you of things to work on."

Convene the class's attention. Tell students that they can accelerate their growth as writers by not only putting into action all they have already learned, but by also aiming to learn new things.

"I see that you are bringing all you've learned to this new project. Good job. You are staying at this nice high level," I said, pointing to the top of the growth curve I'd drawn earlier. "But writers, I want to tell you something else that researchers have found. They have found that after a learner's initial spurt of growth, *this* is what happens." I drew a flat line to show how that initial spike in growth usually levels off.

"What that research shows is that when people learn something—soccer, a video game, information writing—they get better quickly and dramatically, but then . . . they level off. They plateau! The problem is, I want *you* to continue getting even better. Here is the good news. You don't have to plateau." I returned to my earlier sketch of a spurting growth curve, and this time I made the growth spurt up a second time.

❖ **Name the teaching point.**

"Today I want to teach you that the way writers keep their growth curve going up is by not only using all they have already learned, but by also continuing to work to master new things. To do that, writers need to set crystal clear goals for themselves and then to work deliberately to meet those goals."

FIG. 15–1b   Page 2

TEACHING

Guide students to look between a checklist and a mentor text, noticing how the author did what the checklist asks for. Then ask them to use the checklist and mentor text to help plan revisions.

"One way to give yourself goals for getting even better is to study a mentor text and to think, 'How can I improve my text so that it's *that* good? How can I improve myself so I write *that* well?'

"To continue your growth curve, you need some serious new goals to work on this whole week. I'm going to give you a checklist on the qualities of good information writing that people at Teachers College, Columbia University made. You'll see it is divided into parts, and I suggest you read one part of the checklist, then look at the mentor text to see how that author did what is on the checklist. Then you can use both the checklist and the mentor text to help you get ideas for how to improve what you did in that part of *your* writing." I distributed a copy of both the Up the Ladder: Information Writing Checklist and the mentor text to each student. "Let's just look at the first part, the beginning, for now," I said.

Up the Ladder: Information Writing Checklist

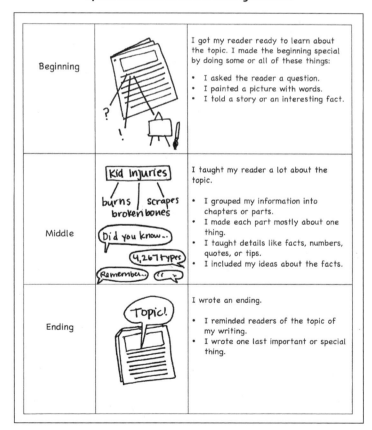

Beginning		I got my reader ready to learn about the topic. I made the beginning special by doing some or all of these things: • I asked the reader a question. • I painted a picture with words. • I told a story or an interesting fact.
Middle	Kid Injuries burns / scrapes broken bones Did you know.. 4,267 types Remember...	I taught my reader a lot about the topic. • I grouped my information into chapters or parts. • I made each part mostly about one thing. • I taught details like facts, numbers, quotes, or tips. • I included my ideas about the facts.
Ending	Topic!	I wrote an ending. • I reminded readers of the topic of my writing. • I wrote one last important or special thing.

This is an adaptation of the checklist in Writing Pathways, *the assessment system that undergirds the larger Units of Study series. If the checklist below feels too easy or too challenging for your students, and you have a copy of* Writing Pathways, *you can adapt the second-, fourth-, or fifth-grade version of the checklist.*

"I'll read the beginning of the mentor text, and will you see if this author has done anything from that section of the checklist?" I read:

Bulldogs Introduction

Have you ever seen a dog whose face is so wrinkled it makes you laugh? That might be a bulldog. I am an expert on Bulldogs because I have one. I am going to tell you everything you need to know about Bulldogs.

"As I reread, think with me. Let's ask and think, 'What did the writer do here? Did the writer do any of the things on the checklist?'" I reread the first paragraph, then asked kids to turn and talk.

I coached into the children's talk:

- "So you notice that the author says 'I am going to teach you . . .' You think that gets the reader ready to learn? Good noticing."

- "You're right! She is asking a question. Why do you think she does that?"

- "You think this could be even better? She could have painted a word picture? You are right. Look to the next paragraph and you'll see it comes a bit later, but she could move that up front, right?"

I gathered the class. "Writers, I love how you noticed that this author got readers ready to learn. You are right that she tells her topic and tries to get readers interested, right?" I pointed to the pertinent sentences and annotated them with a Post-it.

Channel kids to consider how the checklist and mentor text might help them revise the beginning and ending of their own writing.

"Writers, why did we do this?" Hands shot up and, as if anticipating what kids would say, I nodded. "The point is that now you can use the checklist and the mentor text to help you think about big goals for your own writing. You can check out your writing, thinking, 'Did I do that? How could I get even *better*?' I've got new revision plans for our fireworks book. Do you have new plans for your book? Turn and talk, or stop and jot if you prefer."

I made a new Post-it for our fireworks book. I wrote, "No beginning! Get readers ready. Paint a word picture."

Teachers, this piece on bulldogs is from Writing Pathways. *This piece represents the work that, in some ideal world, students who have grown up in a strong writing curriculum should be able to produce by the end of third grade. It's an ambitious goal for third-grade writers.*

Teachers, notice the tagged, annotated text in the online resources and try to replicate some version of that, adding the tags as you talk about each part of the writing.

ACTIVE ENGAGEMENT

Set partnerships up to learn from another part of the same mentor text. Anticipate this will be challenging for kids, so don't expect mastery, but instead, approximation.

"Writers, rise to the challenge of your revision work. Sit up. Focus!" I waited. "You need to do this super-challenging work on your own. We looked together at the part of the checklist that talks about beginnings, but we didn't look at the more important part: the middle. Will you and your partner read the part of the checklist that explains what information writers do in the *middle* of the text, and then study the next two sections of the mentor text to see if the writer does what you see on the checklist? Go!"

The kids settled into this work, and I circulated, coaching. They looked between this and the checklist:

What They Look Like

*One fact about Bulldogs is that they have very unusual looks. They have a short, wide body and short legs. They can be different colors but the most common colors are tan, black, and white. The best part about the Bulldog's looks is its face. The Bulldog has a wrinkled looking face and a wide **jaw**. It looks like it is always sad! But don't worry, that's just its look. It has round black eyes and a short **muzzle**. The biggest Bulldogs weigh about 50 pounds.*

Bulldog Care

*Bulldogs need to be taken care of. It is important for bulldogs to get plenty of exercise. They need to be walked at least once a day. Also, their fur, called the **coat**, can get dirty so they need to be brushed.*

The bulldog needs to eat good food in order to stay healthy. Bulldogs can get fat so it's important to feed them just the amount of food they need. Some kinds of food that are good for bulldogs are special dog food, biscuits, and mashed potatoes.

Bulldogs need to take baths about once every month. My dad says, "You need to wash him so he stays healthy!" But just the bath isn't enough. After the bath you have to clean around their wrinkles because the wrinkles can get dirty. Also they get really smelly!

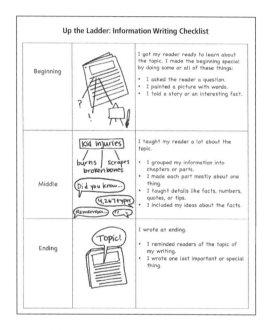

This is especially important. Don't skip it!

"Partners, team up with another nearby partnership and mark up plans for what you can do with your writing." As partners worked, I coached in, especially reminding them that writers "sort the laundry." Did they want to write with a table of contents and turn their pages into chapters?

I coached in with prompts like, "Can you see details like facts, numbers, and quotes in the mentor text? Do you have as many in your text? Does that give you ideas for what you could do next, for goals?" Then I reconvened the group.

"I'm thinking that our fireworks book probably should have chapters," I said. Counting off on my fingers, I said, "Chapter 1: a beginning; Chapter 2: kinds of fireworks; Chapter 3: the danger of fireworks; Chapter 4: July 4th. And maybe another chapter, too."

Coach writers to make revision plans before heading back to independent writing spots.

"Before heading back to your writing spots, will you leave a few more Post-its on your book, containing plans for how you'll take this book from good to great? Remember that you'll want to set ambitious goals for yourself to do work that is better than anything you have ever done—that's how you'll keep your growth curve going up and up," and I pointed to the diagram I'd made earlier.

become famous, ^new paragraph^ if so I. don't let your fans down they love and subscribe to you for a reason. 2. dont be mean, appreciate your subscribers and everyone ~~are~~ around you. 3.

Add in...
a small guide for what to do if you become famous (or something along those lines)

FIG. 15–2   Gigi's revision plan.

Support Some Writers in Making Big Revisions—and Work with Others Who May Need Alternate Mentor Texts and Checklists

Move quickly among the writers, coaching in ways that encourage substantial revisions.

VOICEOVERS TO ENCOURAGE SUBSTANTIAL REVISIONS:

As you move among the students today, you'll want to galvanize kids to put their revision plans into action. You might say:

- **To a student who seems at a loss for what to do:** "Why don't you teach me about your topic, and then we can go from there?" As the child teaches, ask questions. "So if I'm hearing you right, you'd like to add a chapter on X, and a chapter on Y, as you have tons to teach about both of them. And you have a lot more to say about this," pointing to a small comment on one page of the initial draft, "so you'll probably expand this. Does that sound like a plan?"

- **To a student making major revisions:** "Wow! I *love* the way you are revising with scissors as well as a pen. That's very professional. The way you have scissored this apart leaves lots of space for whole new writing, doesn't it?"

- **To a student using the checklist productively:** "I love how you're going step by step down the checklist, and how for each item, you are holding yourself to doing even better work in your draft. Some kids just glance at checklists and think, 'I've done that, I've done that, check, check,' but *you* realize the whole point is to use this as a tool to get stronger. Fabulous work."

- **To a student not finding the checklist immediately helpful:** "You aren't finding a way to use this tool to make your writing better? That's a shame. But there are other ways to push yourself to get stronger as a writer. Take a book you admire and use it almost like a checklist. Study the beginning, then revise yours. Then study the first paragraph, revise yours."

- **To a student reluctant to make major revisions:** "You are warming up by making tiny revisions. Will you start on important, major revisions soon? Let me get you five or six blank sheets of paper for new chapters you're going to want to get going on. What will one new chapter be about?"

SMALL GROUP

Support a small group to use a less—or a more—developed mentor text and checklist.

You might decide to convene a small group that would find it helpful to use a less or a more developed mentor text and checklist than those in this session. The session includes an adaptation of the end-of-third-grade checklist for information writing, and a version of "Bulldogs" that is meant to parallel that checklist. In the online resources, you'll find version of "Bulldogs" at both easier and more challenging levels. (As noted earlier, if you have a copy of *Writing Pathways*, you can adapt the second-, fourth-, or fifth-grade version of the checklist.) In a small group, then, you could channel students to work with a partner and to study one of the alternate texts. The important thing is for kids to be challenged—and to know that with hard work, they can meet the challenge. Either way, you'll set them up to look between the checklist, the mentor text, and most importantly, their writing.

"Writers, I'm seeing some timid revisions and I want to remind you that you will be working for five days on this one book—so you'll be turning your skinny books into big fat books. How many of you are planning to write a nonfiction chapter book, thumbs up?" I nodded. "Great! Are there some of you who are considering writing a single long article, only with subheadings like those in the bulldog piece?" Again, I congratulated that group.

"Either way, try to push yourself to choose more demanding paper. I've laid some new paper choices out in the writing corner. You'll want to choose paper that pushes you to write more in a day than you have ever written before. Remember though, you only want to write on one side of each paper. That will make it easier to cut it up without worrying about the writing on the other side.

"And when it comes to revision, they won't be the tiny little revisions that can be added in with carets! No way! If something doesn't belong where it is, get out the scissors or make giant big cross-outs. Don't be afraid to move information. Get back to work."

As kids worked, I voiced over, "Some of you are getting rid of parts because they are not your best information. This subtraction, this rewriting, this new organizing—this is all brave work, writers. I see the brave, important work you are doing and I salute you."

Help Writers Share and Glory in Their Revisions

Make a big deal about students' brave revision work.

"Writers, I am blown away by you. Lots of kids find it hard to revise. They tack on one extra sentence and call that revision. That's *not* revision. Revision is being willing to see your piece again, with fresh eyes. *You* are doing that. You are being brave. You're doing *large-scale revision*—willing to make big changes.

"Point to a place where you did some brave revision work!" Kids pointed at cross-outs, paper strips, Post-its. "Look at all that determination," I marveled. "Point to another!" Kids pointed to added details or rewritten introductions. "Who can point to a third place? Fabulous!"

WORKING WITH ENL STUDENTS

This session is already very supportive for ENLs:

◆ "Bulldogs" mentor text and "Information Writing Checklist" provide concrete examples with explanations that can be revisited.

◆ Options throughout this session will help writers with varied strengths to feel supported. For example, putting an interesting fact at the beginning of a text is a far easier way to write a strong beginning than the strategy of helping readers picture the topic.

To provide additional support for ENLs you might:

◆ Link today's work to earlier work learned and practiced in Bend II, particularly the structures information writers use by referring to the anchor chart.

◆ You could opt to use a less developed mentor text and checklist.

Information Writers Are Investigators

Conducting Interviews and Taking Surveys

IN THIS SESSION

TODAY YOU'LL teach students that nonfiction writers often gather new information for their books. One way they do this is by asking people questions—in an interview or a survey.

TODAY STUDENTS will continue to work on their information chapter books (made by revising and expanding a Bend 1 book). They will be drafting new chapters and possibly revising those chapters. They can collect more information for their books by doing research.

GETTING READY

✔ Direct partners to bring their copies of the bulldog text to the meeting area (see Connection).

✔ Display chart showing kinds of information in bulldog text (see Connection).

✔ Display the bulldog text and annotate it for kinds of information (see Connection).

✔ Have paper ready to demonstrate how to include direct quotes into a new chapter of your class book (see Teaching and Active Engagement).

✔ Make copies for each student of a short survey on the class topic to demonstrate how to gather data for statistics (see Teaching and Active Engagement).

✔ If you convene a small group on adding additional information, provide copies of book excerpts or articles related to your students' topics (see Conferring and Small-Group Work).

✔ Transcribe parts of a student interview to demonstrate how to include choice bits in an information book (see Share).

✔ Today's minilesson video:

hein.pub/UTLINFO_16

Information Writers Are Investigators
Conducting Interviews and Taking Surveys

CONNECTION

Acknowledge everything that students have put into their information writing. Then tell them that one important thing is missing: other people's knowledge of their topics.

"Writers, when you studied the bulldog mentor text yesterday, I heard many of you commenting on how much information was in that text. You're right. There is a lot of information there—and here's something worth noticing—there are lots of *kinds of* information. By 'kinds of information,' I mean there are not just facts. See if you and your partner can find some of these kinds of information in the bulldog text," I said, channeling them to look just at the two sections of the text, "What they look like" and "Bulldog care."

Many connections in a minilesson are nice warm-ups that can conceivably be skipped if the teacher is short on time, but this is an extremely important message that could easily be the subject of an entire minilesson.

Descriptions	Numbers
Academic vocabulary and definitions	Quotations
Lists	Tips
Examples	Stories

The class had called out examples of kinds of information, and I annotated the sections. "I think some of you are realizing that one goal you might set is to get *more* kinds of information into your writing. That would be a super-wise goal because information writing is made with solid bricks of information—and that information comes as descriptions, vocabulary, lists, and so forth.

Keep up your pace. If a child gives an incorrect answer, do not start a long conversation with that child. Just nod and gesture for more responses. Annotate the correct responses that will help others. Don't try to make a complete document. If you annotate four things, you'll have spent enough time on this.

"Some kids don't know that, so their books are filled with comments like, 'I love *love love* dogs, yes I do,' and 'Have you ever had a dog because you should. They are *great*.' The problem with that kind of writing is that it isn't really information writing because it's missing one thing . . ."

Kids chimed in, on cue, to say it was missing information. Nodding, I affirmed their response. "You're right! Sometimes kids' information books are missing . . . *information!*

"Writers, as you revise your writing and make your Bend I book into a brand-new and much-improved book, you'll write with solid information in your chapters. You'll do this by putting different kinds of information into your chapters. Check the list and think, 'Have I yet added a description?' and so forth."

❖ Name the teaching point.

"Today I want to teach you that one way to get more information on a topic is to draw on the expertise of the people near you. You can interview people, or you can conduct what's called a survey, and that will give you a lot of information on your topic. You can write new chapters or revise existing chapters by adding more information, including the information you learn from surveys and interviews."

TEACHING AND ACTIVE ENGAGEMENT

Demonstrate two ways of gathering information: conducting an interview and taking a survey. Explain that it is best to ask the same question of several sources and that some questions produce more interesting answers.

"Let me show you how you can use interviews and surveys to gather information. First step is to prepare questions. If I want to interview people about fireworks, I think of questions we could ask over and over to a few people. Help me come up with some."

A youngster or two chipped in and soon we had several.

> Where have you seen fireworks in real life?
>
> Have you or anyone you know ever been hurt by fireworks? Scared by them?

I said, "Some questions can help the person being interviewed to think deeply." As I add some to our list, think about equally thoughtful questions you could ask related to the topic of your writing.

> What surprises you about fireworks?
>
> If you could invent a new kind of fireworks, what would it be like?

Sometimes you call on kids and they present wack-a-doodle ideas. There are ways to handle this. First, you might say, quickly and urgently, "Tell each other some questions we could include." Then listen to a kid or two, and only call on one whose answer is reasonable, though it need not match ours exactly. However, listening for the right answer can also take forever, so you can also listen for a sec, then convene the class, saying, "Eyes back here. I heard you saying . . ." and say whatever you wish you'd heard. Don't let yourself get derailed or get into a back-and-forth with one child in the midst of a mini-lesson. You can reach that child later.

Show students how information gleaned from interviews can produce quotations to add to the text. Demonstrate the use of quotations, including the use of punctuation and transitions.

Then I said, "So let me show you how to add the information from interviews into their texts. Let's choose an interview question that could help us write a good beginning to our Fireworks book." Soon I was interviewing Nathan and then Breshna to learn where she had seen fireworks. I turned to a blank page, titled it Chapter 1, and wrote:

> If you have ever seen fireworks, you remember them. Breshna described the first time she saw fireworks by saying, "My parents and I went to the beach to watch them. When it got dark, they shot fireworks up over the water."

When I finished this, I said, "Tell your partner what I did to include the person's exact words into our Fireworks book."

After listening for a minute, I convened the class, underlined the use of transitions, punctuation, and capitals, and then said, "I know you'll do the same. Writers, right now, point to a place in your writing where you think interviewing could help you add in more information."

Press on to a brief overview of surveys. To show students when a person is apt to use a survey instead of an interview, collect statistics on the number of students who . . .

After a few seconds—before everyone had completed this—I pressed on. "I want to show you one more way to collect information for your books. Surveys can help you gather statistics. For example, a survey could allow us to say (and I'm just making this information up for now), 'Fourteen kids in this class have never seen fireworks in real life,' or 'More than half the class would prefer to celebrate July 4th with fireworks than with a picnic.'

"I just made up those numbers but we could get real numbers if you'd be willing to take a little survey I made up last night. You game?" I handed out this survey:

> 1) How many times in real life have you see fireworks?
> ____0 ____1-2 ____3-5 ___more than 5
>
> 2) Which of these fireworks do you like best?
> ____sparklers_____the big flower-like ones____ the rocket-like ones
>
> 3) How would you prefer to celebrate July 4th?
> ___fireworks____a cookout ____a baseball game

"Writers, when you look at this survey, would you think about a question you could ask in a survey related to *your* topic?"

Of course, you can interview your own students to collect quotes on fireworks and use them for your class book.

LINK

Send students off to write, reminding them of the two new information-gathering strategies they learned, which are part of a bigger repertoire.

"Today, you have tons of work to do. I know you haven't half-finished all the things on your to-do list, and that you keep getting new ideas for new chapters you could write. As you work, remember that information writing is composed of concrete specific information. Keep that 'Bulldogs' mentor text close by as a reminder that you can include lots of kinds of information in your books. And keep in mind that interviews and surveys are useful ways to gather information. People use surveys to collect statistics, and conduct interviews to get personal stories and quotes. But writers, do you all need to be interviewing and surveying today? Nope. You could add *any* of the kinds of information to your draft."

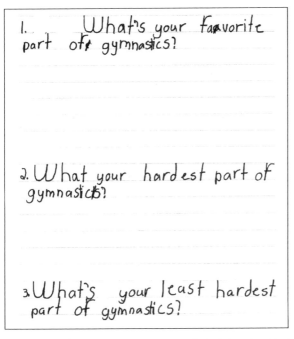

FIG. 16–1   These two writers are ready to interview their classmates.

Support Writers to Keep Paragraphs in Mind and to Use Research to Tap into and Organize More Information

WHEN HELPING WRITERS to work on the two major challenges of information writing—elaboration and structure—you'll see that as writers increase the amount of elaboration in a draft, they end up needing more sophisticated structuring skills. For example, if the writer is writing about the mall and is working on one chapter about the stores on the lower floor of the mall, he may want to quote part of what a friend says about some of those stores. But the friend may well have rambled on to other topics in that same interview, and chances are the writer will end up putting some of those comments into the chapter on the lower floor of the mall. There will be countless examples of this, and so it will be important for you to coach kids to reread their writing, taking out everything that doesn't go. Sometimes this will mean moving information, sometimes deleting. Either way, it will be very important for you to remind them that there are boundaries to what does and does not go into a chapter—and that the same is actually true for a paragraph. The paragraph about Starbucks (at the mall) can't also tell about Macy's, unless it is actually a paragraph about all the stores at the mall.

MID-WORKSHOP TEACHING Encouraging resourcefulness in locating information

"Writers, some of you are telling me that you want to include more information in your writing, but that your classmates may not be good sources. You may need to conduct interviews with people outside of class, in which case you can prepare the questions and make plans in class for interviews that you do outside of class.

"You can also get information from experts who have written about topics. We have a classroom library, a school library, and Internet access. Nothing should stop you from getting the information you need so you can teach readers about your topic."

Collect a small group of students to find additional information and insert it in their information books.

"I gathered you here because it seems that each of your books could get worlds better with more information—but I'm not sure there is an expert on cheetahs or race cars in this class," I said, referencing the students' topics. "So your challenge is to get more information into your book even if the experts aren't close by."

As a response to that challenge, I distributed relevant book excerpts to each writer in the small group. "I've marked parts that especially addresses your topics. Can you work in pairs, helping one writer at a time find one great piece of information to add to his or her book and then figuring out a way to add that information?" I gestured to flaps, Post-its, and colored marker pens. "Then switch off so that everyone gets help." While the kids started this work, I coached:

"Maybe one of you can find where this information could go in Julian's book?"

"How do you think Megan could get that information into her page?"

"You'll need some paper, scissors, and tape."

"Are you planning to quote or to say it in your own words?"

"Remember when you quote to just zoom in on the really good part."

"Here's a model of how another author added a quote to his chapter. Study the tiny details of how he did it."

I left the researchers to continue working without me. Later I told the whole class about what they'd done, inviting others to study their work as a mentor text.

got interviews?
Fireworks can be seen at many different places including lakes, malls, amusement parks and even in your own backyard. In an interview, Nicholle Bingham stated "I usually watch fireworks at the town park in Stamford." July 4th is only one holiday when fireworks can be seen.

INPUT tHEM!!

* don't forget quotation marks
* make sure to include who said it
* take pieces of the interview

got Surveys?
Fireworks have been used as a form of celebration for over 1,000 years. Based off a survey given to fourth grade students, 9 out of 16 students have seen fireworks in real life. I'm sure they have changed over the years.

INPUT tHEM !!!

* don't forget to include how many people took your survey and what you found from it
* make sure it fits in with your facts and flows

SHARE

Mining Interviews for Choice Bits to Include in Writing

Remind students that information writers put only the very best parts of an interview in a book. Invite kids to help decide what they would include from an interview two of them did.

"Writers, when you conduct an interview or when you want to quote from a book, remember that you don't plop a whole half-page quote into your writing. You mine out the gold, you locate the most important, most surprising bits. To practice, let's see if we can help Maria figure out what part of her interview of Jacob would be the best to include in her book on the Second Avenue Subway.

"Maria, can you repeat a bit of your interview for us?" She came to the front of the room, and said to Jacob, "What's the Second Avenue station near your apartment like?"

Jacob repeated the answer he'd given her earlier, saying, "You have to go down an escalator to get there. The platform is really clean 'cause it's new and only the Q train goes there. There are huge murals, as big as the walls. They show famous people. One shows the artist, Kara Walker, with her beautiful, happy hair."

As Jacob talked, I scribed as fast as I could, and now I showed the transcript to the class. "Writers, turn and tell your partner which part of this interview you'd quote. Remember, you can't plop this whole thing in. You can only include small bits. So think, 'Is there a part that feels especially important, or especially interesting?'"

I gave kids just a couple of minutes to talk. I reconvened the class and said, "Many of you said you never heard of a subway station with wall-sized murals, and you thought that was a big deal. So Maria might just quote that part, saying something like, 'Jacob describes the Second Avenue Station is clean "because it is still new."' But it isn't just clean—it also has beauty there. As Jacob said, 'There are big huge murals there, as big as the walls. They show famous people.' Jacob's favorite is a mural showing Kara Walker."

Debrief. Review the process the class just followed to home in on a special part of one child's interview that kids can follow in their own projects.

"Writers, do you see how when you quote from an interview, you pick only a small part—the very best, most important, or surprising part that you know will grab your readers' attention? Right now, look through your own interviews, if you've given one, and see if you can isolate a part like this one."

We model how you might want to do this activity with your class. You'll want to choose two of your own students and use their interview work to demonstrate how to find and use the best parts of an interview in a book.

WORKING WITH ENL STUDENTS

This session is already very supportive for ENLs:

◆ The active engagement sets up kids to work in small groups, providing a chance for them to listen to and process each other's ideas. This time also provides ENLs with strong language models that can help them with questions to use when they interview or survey others.

To provide additional support for ENLs, you might:

◆ List the question words that kids probably know (*who*, *what*, *where*, *why*) to help them generate a few questions to use in their interviews or surveys. Write these questions in a mini-chart for kids to refer to as they work.

Balancing Facts with Thinking

IN THIS SESSION

TODAY YOU'LL teach students that information writers do more than record facts—they reflect on them. For example, they pose questions, make comparisons, and make comments.

TODAY STUDENTS will continue to revise and draft their information books. They will learn how to add their own thoughts to the facts in their books.

GETTING READY

✔ Display the "Bulldogs" mentor text with sentences highlighted to show how the author expressed ideas (see Connection).

✔ Display the "How to Write a Nonfiction Chapter Book" anchor chart for reference to question words (see Teaching).

✔ Prepare a draft of the class book on fireworks, then revise to add ideas (see Active Engagement).

✔ Display the Information Writing Checklist (see Link).

✔ If you confer with a student on paragraphs, provide "un-paragraphed" simple texts (see Conferring and Small-Group Work).

✔ Print copies of "Transitions" chart for each student (see Share).

✔ Today's minilesson video:

hein.pub/UTLINFO_17

Balancing Facts with Thinking

CONNECTION

Call your students' attention to the fact that good information writing is made of information *and* ideas. Show them examples from the mentor text that has threaded through this bend.

"Writers, I want you to look again at our 'Bulldogs' mentor text. This time I'm hoping you'll notice something that none of you commented on earlier. I highlighted two parts. Notice that in both instances, the writer has written not only with information, but also with ideas—with the writer's *thoughts* about the information."

I had highlighted these sections of the mentor text, an enlarged copy of which continued to hang in the front of the classroom.

> *The bulldog has a wrinkled looking face and a wide jaw. <u>It looks like it is always sad! But don't worry, that's just its look.</u>*

> *One fact about bulldogs is that they are very tame. They are good to have around kids and they are good watchdogs. <u>They may look like they are mean, but really they are not. For example, in my book there was a story about a Bulldog who saved his family by barking when there was a fire.</u>*

Tell students an anecdote that sets up your teaching point.

"My point is that when you think about goals to work toward to keep your growth curve high, think about writing not only with information—but also with ideas. Last year, a student of mine wrote about lobsters. She put interesting facts in her lobster book. Listen to this one: some lobsters live to be 100 years old. Fascinating, right? But the problem with her book was that it was *all* facts. It was one fact, then the next, then the next. Fact, fact, fact. The facts came at me so fast that as a reader, I didn't have time to think. And I *wanted* to think. Because the facts were fascinating.

"So I asked her to take each fact and to add her thinking about it. She started with 'Some lobsters live to be 100.' I told her, 'Now think about it. That's a pretty remarkable fact. What does it make you think?'"

You'll note that references to the one "Bulldogs" text thread through many of these minilessons. It is helpful for kids when you work to make one minilesson build upon the next, as this makes them more memorable.

This example actually comes from a graduate student at Teachers College. In graduate courses at Teachers College, adults find that writing information texts is no small challenge! Most grown-ups struggle with the same challenges that kids encounter.

Breaking from the story, I said to students, "Will you try it? 'Some lobsters live to be 100.' Now, say more. Take this one fact and add your thinking." I waited. The students seemed stuck.

"Here is a tip. It's the same one I gave my lobster-writing student last year. It's today's teaching point."

❖ **Name the teaching point.**

"Today I want to teach you that when you want to add your thoughts about the facts that you have included in your writing, it can help to ask and answer questions related to those facts, to make comparisons with other things you know, or to make comments on those facts."

TEACHING

Model how to pause to think about a particularly interesting fact about the class's shared topic.

"Help me do that sort of thinking about 'Some lobsters live to be 100.'

"First: a question. It can help to think of those 'Who, Where, When, Why' questions. Hmm, . . . How about we start by asking . . . who? Lobsters aren't people, so maybe we say *which*? *Which* of the lobsters I've eaten is ninety-seven years old? How can I tell?"

I looked out at the class, pointed to the list of cue words on our anchor chart, *Who? What? Where? Why?*, and asked, "Do you have questions about 'Some lobsters live to be 100'?" One youngster piped up, "Why do they live to be so old? Is it because their shell protects them?" Another asked, "Where do the old lobsters live? Are the ones in Maine old?"

"Let's think about how this fact is the same or different from something we already know. Let's think of ages of animals that we know. Umm, . . . I'm thinking that it is interesting that cats and dogs live to be about ten or twelve, and lobsters live to be 100. The only animals that live that long are lobsters, parrots, and those big tortoises. Interesting.

"My point, writers, is that if we were writing a book about lobsters and we'd written 'Some lobsters live to be 100,' we could we add this sort of thinking to our book, right? Yes!

"What we just did with the fact 'Some lobsters live to be 100' is exactly what you can do with the facts that you write about in your books."

The Flash's big enemy is Savitar. Savitar hates Barry because Barry trapped Savitar in the speed force. The speed force being the force that gave Barry his speed. Since that happened, Savitar tries to make Barry's life awful.

Savitar is also evil because he hurt one of Barry's teammates, Iris. Barry also got hurt by Savitar, as well as Wally who got trapped in the speed force by Savitar.

Why does Savitar do all of this? Because he doesn't care who he hurts. When I asked Cara the question, "Who is your least favorite character in The Flash?" She said, "Savitar. Because he's out to get The Flash and everyone he cares for."

Savitar hates Barry, so the Flash has to work hard to keep himself and his teammates safe from Savitar.

FIG. 17–1   Maria balances facts with thinking *and* includes a quote from her interview.

ACTIVE ENGAGEMENT

Set partners up to try this work, with each duo tackling a particular piece of information on the class topic.

"Ready to give this a go yourselves? Here are a few pieces of information you helped me learn about our topic, 'Fireworks.'" I pointed to a passage from our draft that brimmed with facts.

When Do You Watch Fireworks?

The 4th of the July is the US's birthday. Since 1777, this country has celebrated with fireworks. Sometimes the fireworks are red, white, and blue, or look like a flag, or spell USA, and sometimes, patriotic music is played at the same time. But often the fireworks are not extra patriotic, just extra grand. AND they cost more than $20,000. Less than half of the kids in this class watch fireworks on July 4th.

"There's a lot of solid information here, but it feels a bit like the reader is being pelted with facts: bam, bam, bam. There are no thoughts about those facts, no ideas or insights about them.

"Will you front-row partners add thinking to this passage by asking and answering a question? Second-row partners, do the same by adding a comparison. Third-row writers, make a comment about a fact or two. Ready? Go!"

As partners talked, I circled the rows, listening in and jotting their questions, comparisons, and comments. Then I reconvened the group. "Wow. I heard you say such cool things. I'm going to try to include a lot of what I heard in a revision—and you'll see me go from facts to ideas, from what is written here to new stuff we could add."

I read the existing passage aloud, and after many sentences, added one (writing-in-the-air only to save time) that captured thoughts, a few of which I'd heard from the kids.

When Do You Watch Fireworks?

The 4th of the July is the US's birthday. Since 1777, places celebrate with fireworks. <u>That means people have celebrated July 4th with fireworks for almost 250 years—but no one thinks of fireworks as old-fashioned. They have probably changed a lot since 1777!</u>

Sometimes the fireworks are red, white, and blue, or look like a flag, or spell USA, and sometimes, patriotic music is played at the same time. But often the fireworks are not extra patriotic, just extra grand. <u>Just like people sometimes forget the religious part of Christmas and just think of it as a time to get presents, people sometimes forget the real reason</u> for celebrating July 4th.

AND they cost more than $20,000. <u>I could compare that amount of money with the amount it costs to feed a lot of homeless people. It makes me wonder if shooting fireworks is the best way to celebrate the US's birthday.</u> Less than half of the kids in this class watch fireworks on July 4th.

Debrief. Remind students that it pays off to add thinking to facts in information writing.

"Writers, anytime you find yourself writing fact after fact after fact, challenge yourself to pause and add your thinking. Thoughtful questions, comments, and comparisons can do a lot to engage a reader."

LINK

Send children off to write and suggest that one thing they might try is adding their thinking about a particularly interesting fact.

"As you go off to write today, know that adding in your thinking is one of many things you might try. Certainly, if you reread a page in your book and find that it's fact-fact-fact, you may want to pose a question or put in your reaction to one or more of those facts.

"I also want to point out," I said as I placed the Information Writing Checklist under the document camera, "that 'I included my ideas about the facts' is a part of the Information Writing Checklist. Now you know how to do that. Off you go!"

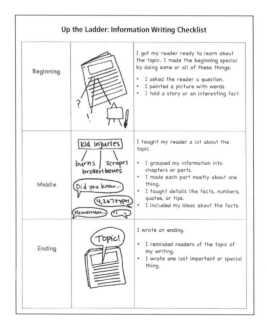

Support Students as They Revise and Grow Their Information Books

ONE WAY TO PREPARE for conferring and small-group work is to think about the minilesson of the day and the work you are channeling kids to do—and to imagine the less-than-perfect ways kids will respond. A second way is to pull in and carry forth the teaching you have done during the last few days, not just today. Expect that today, your children will be adding information from interviews, surveys, and book research into their writing, as well as thinking about that information. They may also be looking at the beginnings and endings of their book and their chapters or subsections. We refer to this as building a "repertoire" of strategies.

Coach Students for Revision, Elaboration, and Adding More Information Effectively	
If . . .	**Then you may want to say . . .**
Students add more without reconsidering the organization of their book, just sticking the new content at the bottoms of their pages.	"I love that you are adding so much into this text. Congratulations. That is very grown-up. "But one person once said that when you reach a mountaintop, ahead of you, you'll see . . . a new mountain. And this super-important work you have done now means that you really need to get some strong organizing muscles. "Because the way your chapters go now, they feel sort of like this: blue, red, blue, green, red, blue. And you will want it to go like this: blue-blue-blue, red-red-red, green-green. That is, you need to sort the laundry all over again. I'll help you to scissor this apart, and then you can make piles of stuff that goes together. It is almost like you need to divide your chapters into chapters."
The "ideas" that children are adding into their draft are just superficial "chitchat," such as "I think that's cool!" or "Isn't that disgusting?"	"You have taken an important step forward. Before you just had fact, fact, fact. Now you have fact, your feelings about that fact, fact, your feelings about the fact. Congratulations. "I think you are now ready to go even a step farther. This next step is going to make a *big* difference. You willing? "My suggestion is that instead of adding your feelings about the information, you actually add your *thinking*, your theories. So if you say, 'Dogs eat a cup of dry food in the morning and at night,' instead of saying 'That's weird' or 'gross,' you need real thoughts. You might get yourself started on having thoughts by using some of these sentences: "The interesting thing about that is . . . "I wonder why . . . Maybe it is because . . . "I'm surprised that . . . because I would have thought . . . "I can compare this to . . . That makes me think . . .'"
Students squish their added writing in between the lines of their texts, making their additions very abbreviated.	"You know how you often outgrow clothes—your pants, your shoes. Well, you are outgrowing your revision tools. You are doing such advanced and ambitious revision that you need tools that are as grown-up as the work you are doing. I'm going to equip you with scissors, paper strips, tape, and these giant Post-its because I can see that you need space for important revisions."

MID-WORKSHOP TEACHING   Helping Each Other Add More Thinking into Drafts

"Writers, how many of you have been adding thinking into your writing?" Many students signaled that they had done so. I acted like I was almost falling over in astonishment that so many of them had done that. "Wow! I am stunned. Today's minilesson was a super-advanced one, and I am blown away that so many of you have actually been doing that important work. Right now, will you get together with your partner and maybe another partnership, and if one of you has done this in a way that you think works, will you show it to the others? Then will you help each other find places to do this work?

"This is *not* easy, so turn your brains on high and get to work."

After a few minutes I intervened, suggesting that writers go back to working alone, even if they hadn't yet had a chance to get and give help.

If a student is still not dividing chunks of text words into paragraphs . . .

- Provide guided practice through the "un-paragraphed" version of a simple text (example below). Coach writers to notice and point out where the topic changes.

> When you skateboard you need a lot of safety gear. You need a helmet to wear on your head. It protects your brain and face. You need to wear elbow pads and kneepads. There are lots of places to go skateboarding. You can go to a parking lot or in your driveway. You can go to a skateboard park too.

- Direct children to take out their own writing and notice where they start teaching something new about their topic or subtopic.

- Voice over as students work:

  - "Is what you're teaching in this part of the page different from what you're teaching on this other part?"

  - "I see you made a new paragraph, great job! It's only one sentence. Add more sentences about that topic."

  - "Look through your entire book for places where the topic changes. And if you find small paragraphs, add on more."

Adding Transition Words to Bring Out Connections and to Say More

Channel students to use transition words to smooth out shifts from one paragraph to another.

"Writers, pretty soon our unit will be over, so it is getting time for you to think about the finishing touches you can add to your writing. I'm going to change the subject from the work you have been doing today to talk to you about your paragraphs. How many of you are writing in paragraphs?"

Most of the children signaled that they were. "Hurrah!" I said. "That is a *huge* accomplishment. And if any of you aren't yet paragraphing, get help from someone, reread your draft, and add a pilcrow," I drew a paragraph sign, "wherever you think a new paragraph belongs.

"Because you are writing in paragraphs, I want to add one tip that can take your paragraphs from good to great. When you shift to a new paragraph, it is often helpful to put some 'tape' into your text to show the reader that the new paragraph still goes with the one before it. Only you don't really use tape, you use *transition words*. I've got a chart to teach you about transition words. This chart has lots of white space for you to add to it—I only filled it in partway. Will you and your partner study the chart? In a moment I am going to give you a pop quiz to see how well you can use this chart to make writing go from good to great." I showed them the "Transitions" chart.

"So if Jeremy wrote, 'The mall has two floors. On the bottom floor . . .' and then he told about that floor, and *now* he wants to tell about the top floor, what transition might he use to start that paragraph?"

Kids called out, "above it," "near it," and "on the other hand."

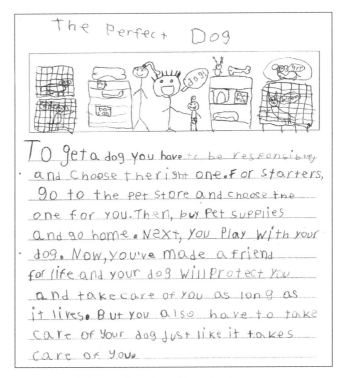

FIG. 17–2   Maia uses time transitions to elaborate.

"If Jeremy wants to describe how he wanders around the mall in one paragraph, and then in another paragraph, tell about having meals at the mall, how might he start the paragraph about having meals?"

Kids called out, "after," "next," and "then."

"Right now will you look at your paragraphs and see if you could use some transitions? The most important place to use them is at the start of your paragraphs. Help each other."

WORKING WITH ENL STUDENTS

This session is already very supportive for ENLs:

◆ In the teaching section, you illustrate the power of the strategy (ask a question, make a comparison, make a comment) by providing an example of the text before and after the revisions are added.

◆ The class book begun by the teacher and revised by students provides support for language and the writing process.

To provide additional support for ENLs, you might:

◆ Create a chart with visuals "Ask a question, make a comparison, make a comment" for students to refer to as they continue to revise their own writing.

◆ Annotate the revised class book so students can visualize where the revisions are.

Transitions

Time words
before, earlier, after, then, next, later, a minute later

Sequence
suddenly, once in awhile, sometimes, often, usually

Place words
nearby, around the corner, on the other side, above it

Comparing words: Things That are the Same
in the same way, similarly

Ranking
more importantly, most importantly, especially, even more important, equally important

Studying Mentor Texts to Create a Revision Plan

IN THIS SESSION

TODAY YOU'LL teach your students that information writers improve their writing by studying the work of great writers and aiming to emulate it.

TODAY STUDENTS will revise their own writing by studying several nonfiction texts that illustrate different craft moves.

GETTING READY

✔ Distribute copies of a passage from a nonfiction text with good examples of craft moves. We chose *A Seed Is Sleepy* by Dianna Hutts Aston (see Teaching).

✔ Create a "Craft Moves Great Information Writers Make" chart to record student responses (see Teaching).

✔ Make sure that each table has large Post-its for revision work (see Active Engagement).

✔ Gather some nonfiction mentor texts for students to consult as inspiration for their own writing. We use passages from *Your Guide to Electricity and Magnetism* by Gill Arbuthnott and *Skunks* by Sandra Markle (see Link and Conferring and Small-Group Work).

✔ Today's minilesson video:

hein.pub/UTLINFO_18

Studying Mentor Texts to Create a Revision Plan

CONNECTION

Explain that information writers can make any topic interesting. Set partners up to study how authors can make kids interested in texts about things like exclamation marks and chickens.

"Writers, I know many of you are trying to put things in your books that will interest your readers, and I love that effort. But the *really* famous nonfiction writers—I mean, the really, *really* famous information writers—can take any ol' topic and make it interesting. The most famous nonfiction writers in the world have written about topics that sound boring at first, like exclamation marks, chickens, warts, and even toilets. And they make those topics interesting!

"I'm not kidding. Do you want to see a little of that Very Famous Writing? One of America's most famous novelists, F. Scott Fitzgerald, once wrote this about exclamation marks":

> *Cut out all those exclamation points. An exclamation point is like laughing at your own joke.*

"That's just two sentences—but it's writing that has lasted a hundred years. It isn't writing for kids. It is super-famous writing for adults. What has F. Scott Fitzgerald done to make this bit of writing about an exclamation mark interesting? Will you and your partner try to figure that out?"

The kids talked, and I circulated, taking notes. Then I reconvened the class. "Some of you said that his writing sounds like he is talking. It sounds like normal, spoken language—and I think you are right. Often when we read great written language, the words on the page almost *ask* to be read aloud, to be said aloud. They have the tempo, the feel, of spoken language. You can practically see F. Scott Fitzgerald gesturing with his hand as he speaks, trying to wipe those exclamation marks off the page. 'Cut those out.'

"I heard some of you say he also uses a comparison, and you are right. It isn't a usual one—like 'soft as cotton.' But when I read it, I thought, 'Yep, that's exactly right.'

"My point is not just that a great writer can make something as simple as an exclamation mark interesting. It's also that you and I can learn from writing that others have done. And I don't mean we can learn about exclamation marks. We can learn about great writing."

This is an important point to be making so late in the unit—but the good news is that students will experience other units and will continue to study how to write information texts well.

Always remember that there is little gained from big, long examples. Make your point as briefly as you can because always, the goal is to save time for kids' own important writing.

✣ Name the teaching point.

"Today I want to remind you that writers study other great writers, and they let that writing influence their writing. That's as true for writers of information books as it is for any other kind of writer."

TEACHING

Read aloud from a nonfiction text and ask children to signal when they notice something that could influence their own writing. Then have kids turn and talk about what the author did in that part.

"Yesterday I read about thirty nonfiction books, looking for a writer that I thought we could especially learn from. I found an author that I didn't know until yesterday—Dianna Hutts Aston. Let's read a bit of her work to notice things she has done that can make us think, 'Whoa, that could influence my writing!'"

I distributed copies of a passage. "I will read this section from *A Seed Is Sleepy*. I'll read it twice. As you listen, will you underline parts that stand out and begin thinking, 'What has this author done that might influence my writing?'" I read just the first four lines, reading the passage twice, pausing deliberately so that youngsters could *ooh* and *ahh* and in general, have reactions to the text.

> *A seed is sleepy.*
>
> *It lies there, tucked inside its flower, on its cone, or beneath the soil. Snug. Still.*
>
> *To find a spot to grow, a seed might leap from its pod, or cling to a child's shoestring, or tumble through a bear's belly.*
>
> *A seed hopes to land where there is plenty of sunlight, soil, and water.*
>
> *(from* A Seed Is Sleepy *by Dianna Hutts Aston)*

After the second reading, I paused and said, "Whew. The author has done a *lot*, hasn't she? Now, time for the most important job. You need to think, 'What, exactly, did the author of this passage do that I could try in my writing?'" Then I added, "As you talk about this text, don't talk just about seeds—try to find the words to name *how* the author wrote, the craft moves she used that you could try. Turn and talk."

I circulated, listening in, offering quick coaching tips.

- "I hear you say 'I like this part.' Say more. Use as many words as you can to explain what the author did and why it works. What specifically did she do that you could try?"

- "Try to say more. Yes, the author uses one-word sentences—but how do those sentences make the writing better?"

- "Look not just at what the author did in one place. What did she do in more than one place?"

Call for selected students to share. Scaffold students into naming sophisticated craft moves that they might have noticed but might not be able to name yet.

"Wow, you noticed a lot! Even more than I noticed! Let's hear from three of you. Max? Jasmin?" I called on the few kids who I'd heard noticing concrete craft moves.

"She pretended the seed has a feeling—'cause seeds don't really have hope," offered Max.

"She used one-word sentences," shared Jasmin. When I gestured for her to say more, she added, "That makes the one word really important—it made me think and feel more about the seed."

I added, "I also heard some of you say that she 'told a whole bunch of ways that the seed traveled'—giving a list. And she made that travel seem exciting—the seed could travel on a child's shoestring or in a bear's belly."

"Writers, if we think back to both the texts we have studied today—the one about the exclamation mark and this one, you have found a lot of things that writers do. Let's list them." I revealed a chart on which a few of these were already written, and with reminders of what we'd discussed, I added more.

If no child in your room articulated a single craft move, don't despair. Continue as if they did, naming the moves you "think you heard" and don't let this destroy the pacing of the mini-lesson. Later today, you may want to confer with specific children, coaching them to name some of the easier, more obvious craft moves.

ACTIVE ENGAGEMENT

Ask students to study their own writing, noticing where they might revise parts under the influence of the mentor writing, then begin to revise their writing.

"Writers, will you open your writing to a page that you think you might be able to revise under the influence of the texts we have studied so far?" I left a minute for them to do that. "When you find a page for revision, think about what you might do on your page that one of these great writers did. Then, get started. Do the revision right here, right now. I left Post-its at your tables, and you can write on those if you need more space. Get started, writers."

LINK

Send writers off to revise their writing under the influence of one of the mentor texts set out around the room—or under the influence of the mentors the class studied earlier.

"Writers, this work that you have begun, you can do again and again as a writer. Any time you're looking for ways to make your writing even better, you can study what great writers have done, and then let that influence your writing. To support you in that work, I have set out some mentor texts around the room. You might choose to spend some of your workshop time studying what those writers have done and letting it influence your writing. The important thing is that today is your last day to revise your writing. Tomorrow I'm going to ask you to begin editing it."

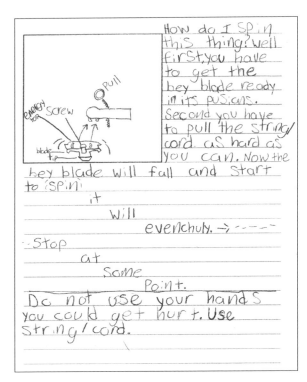

FIG. 18–1   Jasmin applies Sandra Markle's descriptive prose to her chapter on Christmas food.

FIG. 18–2   Nicholas crafts the placement of his text on the page just like mentor author Diana Hutts Aston.

Gaining Inspiration from Other Authors

YOU MIGHT CREATE little author centers in corners of your classroom, inviting your writers to spend a bit of time in one author center before moving to another. In one corner, the youngster will find this passage from *Your Guide to Electricity and Magnetism* by Gill Arbuthnott:

> *Empty Space*
>
> *Atoms are much too small to see . . . Guess what? It turns out most of an atom is just empty space. That is a hard thing to imagine—go ahead, just try to imagine emptiness!*
>
> *Picture the whole atom as being the size of a small island. Sitting in the middle of it is a coconut. That's the nucleus, or the center of the atom. Now imagine tiny mosquitoes flying around the coconut. These are* **electrons**. *The rest of the island is empty!*

MID-WORKSHOP TEACHING Trying Out What Published Authors Do

"Writers, you've been noticing so many things in the mentor texts at your tables. Some of you have discovered the same things we saw F. Scott Fitzgerald do in that excerpt about exclamation marks. Others of you have spotted some of the techniques we saw at play in *A Seed Is Sleepy*. And a few kids have even noted craft moves this class hasn't discussed. Bravo for looking so closely!

"But remember, your job is to revise under the influence of these authors. So if you haven't started doing that, take out your writing, read it over, and find spots where you can try out some of these moves!"

Of course, your students will have written about entirely different subjects: the mall, video games, soccer. It will take them a little while to realize what Arbuthnott's text can teach them, even if their writing has nothing to do with atoms. Different writers will draw different lessons from the mentor text. You could help one to talk to her reader, saying things like "Guess what?" or "Go ahead." You'll want your students to innovate other ways to talk to readers, and it will help if you can imagine other ways yourself. You may want to suggest that writers could say, "Try this," or "Stop and think for a minute."

Another writer might learn entirely different lessons from the same text. Arbuthnott has done a wonderful job describing something, and that is something your students could try. Notice that the mentor text uses comparisons to help readers picture the subject. The author takes special care to help readers imagine the size of the subject.

In another center, students can take lessons from another text. One that we suggest is this snippet from *Skunks* by Sandra Markle:

> *It's a warm July night in a northern Wisconsin forest. A female striped skunk pokes her head out of the hollow log where she has spent the day. After sniffing the air, she looks around for any sign that a predator is lurking nearby. Then she climbs out of the log and sets off in search of a meal, waddling slowly on her short legs. She's about the size of a chubby house cat and getting fatter by the day. The skunk doesn't go very far before she stops to nibble. First, she eats some leaves and fresh green buds. Then she pounces on a spider and eats it. A little further on, her sharp sense of smell leads her to an earthworm underneath the leaf litter covering the forest floor. The sturdy claws of her front paws are designed for digging. She uncovers the worm and eats this juicy mouthful. Then she waddles on.*

Again, your writers will take their own lessons. One might note the power that comes from telling a story in the middle of an information book. Another may notice the strong action words. The way the author brings the subject to life with descriptions that include comparisons. The amount of detail. Remember, it is important for youngsters to use as many words as possible to talk about what they admire. Simply saying "detail" doesn't help the writer much. You might say, "What does the writer notice about the detail? I notice that the details the author describes are those that the skunk might be apt to notice. They are at her eye level, and things are described as she might see them: the earthworm under the leaf litter, the fresh green buds. I notice, too, that this skunk waddles all through the passage." Help your youngsters to look with equal care and to revise their writing to add similar special touches.

Peers Can Be Mentors for Each Other

Channel students to learn from their mentor author-classmates, then to revise their writing under their influence.

"Writing partners, will you get your writing and sit with another partnership at a table? Don't leave anyone out; you can have four, five, or six kids." Once the class had settled into this configuration, I said, "Earlier today we studied the work of mentor authors that I found in our library. You looked really closely at the beauty in those authors' writing. Then you said, 'I can try the same thing,' and you did.

"Now I'm going to ask the writer sitting closest to the windows to select a bit of your writing that you are especially proud of. Lay it out on the tables so everyone in your group can see it. Take half a minute to locate that passage and display it.

"Can you guess what I'm going to suggest? Yes! You can now study the work of another mentor author—your classmate. Talk with your group about what you admire that the author has done on that page. In a few minutes, I'm going to stop the talk and channel you to revise."

The writers talked. Then I said, "All of you except the mentor authors, revise under the influence of that mentor author. You just have three minutes to improve your writing based on something you admire. Mentor authors, you can move around giving the writers in your groups tips."

Once this was done, I said, "If we had more time, I'd love to study the work of every writer in the class. Each and every one of you can look at the best part of your own writing, and try to write that well on every page. You can be your own mentor author!"

WORKING WITH ENL STUDENTS

This session is already very supportive for ENLs:

◆ Students can refer to their own copies of the mentor text when they are drafting or revising.

◆ The think-alouds that you do in the teaching portion of this minilesson provide lots of possible suggestions for how students may revise.

To provide additional support for ENLs, you might:

◆ Provide additional mentor texts with clear examples of comparison and description annotated for students to read.

Deliberate Punctuation

Commas

IN THIS SESSION

TODAY YOU'LL teach students that information writers use commas in deliberate ways—with items in a list, after transition words, and before adding the definition of a technical word.

TODAY STUDENTS will edit their writing to prepare for publication, including fixing paragraphing and run-ons and adding commas.

GETTING READY

✔ Display a sentence without commas and then the same sentence with commas (see Teaching).

✔ Distribute copies of a passage ("Rays, sharks, tuna . . .") to kids (see Teaching).

✔ Display the "Commas are used . . ." chart to students (see Teaching).

✔ Distribute copies of a passage ("Deep-sea fish live . . .") to kids and also display it (see Active Engagement).

✔ Display the "New and Improved Editing Checklist" (see Link).

✔ Display the "Ways Information Writers Use Commas" chart (see Link).

✔ Distribute information books around the meeting area for students to use as mentors for preparing their books for the end-of-unit celebration (see Mid-Workshop Teaching).

✔ Today's minilesson video:

hein.pub/UTLINFO_19

Deliberate Punctuation
Commas

CONNECTION

Suggest that writers have the power—and responsibility—to control the movement of their reader's eyes through deliberate punctuation.

"Writers, tomorrow is the big celebration of your information writing! Today you'll be working to make your writing presentable. Wash its face. Brush its teeth. In other words, it's time to go through your writing sentence by sentence, word by word, eyeballing your spellings, catching those run-ons, fixing those paragraphs, taking charge of punctuation." I gestured to the editing chart the kids already knew from earlier in the unit.

You are harkening back to an earlier editing session, and in using the metaphor from earlier, you are also reminding kids of the editing checklist they already know well.

"Before you even try to do that, I want to remind you of an important point. As a writer, you have some power over your reader. *You* decide where you want your reader to pause and breathe, where you want your reader to raise his voice or change his voice. And where it's okay for the reader to take a break. *You* choose where your reader feels shocked and where your reader asks a question. Punctuation is not the boss of you. *You* are the boss of *it*. It is your tool, just like your pencil and your paper are your tools. You have the power to use punctuation in important ways.

"But have you heard the saying 'With great power comes great responsibility'? It is your responsibility not to leave the reader hanging, not to give the reader an eye-ache. Because if you don't use punctuation appropriately, that's exactly what happens—the reader's eye (and mind!) will feel confused because it will keep moving back over your words, trying to find a signal from you for where to pause, where to stop, what meaning to make."

❖ Name the teaching point.

"Today I want to teach you that writers use punctuation on purpose. In particular, writers use commas as a tool to control their reader's eyes. Writers decide how the reader's eyes should move over their words. They use commas to make the reader pause from taking in more and more words, and to make the reader stop and breathe before looking again."

TEACHING

Invite children to notice that comma omission often results in content that is undecipherable.

"Let me show you what I mean. Read this sentence silently, and tell me how your eyes feel":

> Rays sharks tuna trout cod and eels are all differ-
> ent kinds of fish.

"Nod if *your* eye was as confused as mine. I found my eye jumping back to the words, trying to separate the names of the fish. I'm confused whether there are three fish or four or five—or six.

"Now look at this same sentence, where the writer has used punctuation to help our eyes." I placed the following sentence next to the first one, under the document camera, for children to consider:

> Rays, sharks, tuna, trout, cod, and eels are all dif-
> ferent kinds of fish.

"Tell your partner what the writer did to help your eyes in this second sentence." I gave partners a moment to speak.

"I heard some of you say the commas helped separate the names of fish in that list. I'm glad that you're noticing the importance of the comma. It's a tiny little mark, but it helps the reader's eye see structure."

Channel students into an inquiry into the use of commas in information writing.

"Now I'm going to pass around a piece of information writing that uses commas in different ways. As I read aloud, notice whenever a comma appears, and circle it. In a minute, you'll work with a partner to figure out what role the comma is playing in each instance. Pens ready?" I displayed the following passage and began reading, pausing meaningfully at each comma so children would notice and circle it.

> Rays, sharks, tuna, trout, cod, and eels are all different kinds of fish.
> Fish may live in rivers, lakes, oceans, and streams. Most fish live near
> the surface where sunlight can enter. However, some are **deep-sea**
> **fish**, those that live in the dark depth. Of these, the most common
> are **lantern fish**, or fish that glow in the dark like a lantern. No fish,
> however, can live below five miles.

You'll note that the teaching method in this session is inquiry. There isn't the usual time for demonstration.

"Okay, I see lots of circled commas on your papers. But not each comma you found is doing the same job. Look at the commas with your partner and figure out: What are the commas doing? How is it helping in each case?" As children talked, I displayed the following chart, as if I'd made it from recording their observations.

> Commas are used . . .
> - To separate items in a list
> - Around transition words
> - Before an in-sentence definition

"Writers, how many of you found the commas that separate the items in a list?" I pointed to the first bullet. "What about around transition words—do you see transitions like *however* and *of these* in this piece? Do you see a comma after those words? Some of you noticed that a comma is also used right after bolded words. The important thing about those words is that they are then defined, and the comma is used right before the author adds the definition. Did you all find that?"

ACTIVE ENGAGEMENT

Invite children into the shared reading of a text where they work to insert commas and other punctuation in purposeful ways.

"Right now, I've got a paragraph that is in dire need of some comma work." I handed out copies and displayed the following passage. "In a second, you're going to consult your partner to decide where commas might be added, but before you do, remind yourself of the three places where commas are often used that we just discovered." I pointed to the "Commas are used . . ." chart and motioned for children to begin talking.

> Deep-sea fish live where no sunlight enters. Therefore many have eyes that are large sensitive and help them see in the dark. However some deep-sea fish are totally blind. Many are **bioluminescent** which means they produce their own light.

"Writers, I heard lots of deliberation just now. Thumbs up if you put in a comma after the transition words *therefore* and *however*. Good for you. Was there a hard word that was followed by a definition? Thumbs up if you placed a comma before the definition. Did you see a list in there too? Where?" As students called out possible places, I added the commas accordingly.

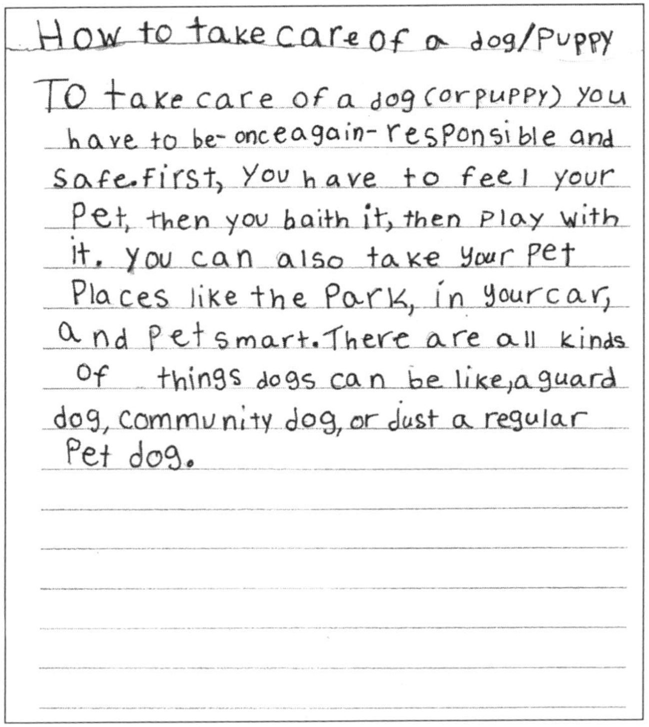

How to take care of a dog/Puppy

TO take care of a dog (or puppy) you have to be -once again- responsible and safe. First, you have to feel your pet, then you baith it, then Play with it. You can also take your pet Places like the Park, in your car, and Petsmart. There are all kinds of things dogs can be like, a guard dog, community dog, or Just a regular Pet dog.

FIG. 19–1 Commas make all the difference to the reader as this piece demonstrates.

LINK

Remind writers to use the now-familiar editing checklist to edit their books, pointing out the brand-new bullet on comma use.

"Writers, you already know this tool that we bring out whenever we ready ourselves for publication." I pointed to the "New and Improved Editing Checklist."

"You already know to watch out for run-ons, and spellings, and to make paragraphs." I ran my finger down the items on the checklist. "But there's a new bullet on your checklist." I pointed again. "It reminds you that commas are not little accidental marks. They are a very powerful tool a writer uses to help the reader's eye. You use them to . . ." I let my voice trail away, holding up a finger as if to count. Children piped in, "to separate items in a list!" I nodded and kept counting, "and after any transition word and also, just before the definition of a technical word." I stopped counting. "I look forward to seeing deliberate punctuation in your sentences. Off you go!"

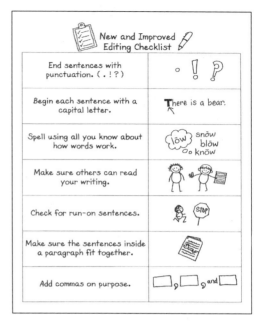

Ways Information Writers Use Commas

Information Writers Use Commas to...	Examples
To separate items in a list	Some kinds of food that are good for bulldogs are special dog food, biscuits, and mashed potatoes.
Around transition words	Next,_____ For example, in my book there was a story about a Bulldog who saved his family by barking when there was a fire.
Before an in-sentence definition	☐, definition Their fur, called the coat, can get dirty so they need to get brushed.

Supporting Self-Editing and Peer Editing

YOU'LL SUPPORT CHILDREN in getting ready for publication today. This does not mean that children spend endless time rewriting their books to be flawless and impeccable. It *does* mean that they keep revising and editing with independence. As you walk around, you might help children decide on the pages that are indeed so fraught with crossed-out words and rewritten sentences that they simply need to be rewritten to be legible. But coach them also to salvage pages or even paragraphs that do not need a major rewrite.

Peer editing will continue to serve children well. Have partners read their writing aloud to each other, pausing wherever the syntax feels awkward and needs rewording. Set peers to catch each other's run-ons and comma omissions.

Take account of sight words or tier 1 words that you see students misspelling. Rather than fixing the error for the student, put these words on the word wall and channel kids to consult this word wall.

Continue to support children who struggle with spelling, coaching them to tap out syllables and to stretch each syllable to hear the sounds inside it. Remind them that there is at least one vowel in each syllable. Also coach them to try spelling a word more than one way. "Try swapping an *s* for an *e* or an *ai* for an *ay*," you might suggest. And, of course, your classroom is full of environmental print that can support kids in spelling with greater accuracy. A word of caution: Remember that dictionaries are for definitions, not spelling, so leave them on the shelf for this work.

MID-WORKSHOP TEACHING Using Mentor Texts to Help Prepare for Publication

"Writers, finish the line or section that you are editing and find me with your eyes." I waited. "I appreciate the way you are putting your pencils down and refocusing our attention. I'd like you to make your way to the meeting area. I know that isn't usual, but it is important."

Once the children had settled, I distributed a pile of information books to each corner of the meeting area.

"You'll see that I'm distributing some information books to you and the writers near you. The reason I'm doing this is that we'll be publishing the day after tomorrow, and you have just a little time left today, plus tomorrow, to get ready. This time, we are celebrating the entire unit, so it is a big deal.

"This might be a good time for you to look again at mentor texts. Notice ways that authors fix up their books for publication: dedications, 'about the author' sections, blurbs on the back cover, anything else that you think matters. Tell each other your ideas for how you could get your book ready for publication. Then get to work. Finish your editing, and start fixing up and fancying up your book."

Polishing Writing for Publication

Encourage students to seek help from their peers to make their books the best they can be.

"Writers, there are times to share and times to *not* share. The day before an author celebration is a good time to *not* share. Keep your book hidden away so that tomorrow you can surprise people with it.

"So today, our share time is not a share, but this can be a time to get help. Every author knows that before a book goes to press, a team of people comes in to help the author. There are illustrators, fact checkers, editors, people who help with marketing. You deserve to have someone help you with your book, too, so during these final moments of this final writing day, don't hesitate to go to anyone and ask for any sort of help you need. You can also ask me for help, if there's something I can do."

The room was soon filled with kids seeking help from classmates with editing and illustrations.

WORKING WITH ENL STUDENTS

This session is already very supportive for ENLs:

◆ The "Ways Information Writers Use Commas" chart in the link offers specific examples on how to use commas.

To provide additional support for ENLs you might:

◆ Provide copies of "personal word walls" with a list of words that children are using repeatedly in their books.

Dressing Up Your Writing

ear Teachers,

You launched this third and final bend by inviting your students to take a Bend I book from good to great. You may have felt some doubt at the beginning of this bend, wondering how exactly your students would manage a week of instruction dedicated to revision. Today is all about celebrating your students' growth and perhaps, more importantly, about celebrating the risks they have taken. It takes a great deal of courage to show up each day with the goal of outgrowing your best work.

MINILESSON

We imagine that you will divide today's workshop into two parts. During the first half of the workshop, students will continue to work on dressing up their writing in preparation for the celebration. You could gather your writers on the rug and quickly share their findings from yesterday's study of mentor texts.

You could share that:

- "About the author" pages often include a summary of the author's education, with some details about the person's life—and sometimes include a funny little story that explains the author's interest in the topic of his or her book.

- Book blurbs usually have a short summary of the book so that readers know what to expect, a direct address to readers to invite them into the topic, a little story about the topic that sets the stage for what's to unfold in the book.

- Dedications are, above all, short! Often they simply list the name of one person the writer wishes to acknowledge.

Before sending your writers off, remind them that they have a limited amount of time (we suggest twenty minutes) to finish fancying up their writing. You may decide to support your writers with pacing by letting them know when they've got ten more minutes to work, five more minutes, and one final minute to dress up their writing.

As kids work, you might voice over reminders: "Don't spend too long on any one part! If you've written your 'about the author' page, move on to your book's blurb . . . or the dedication!" "If you're stuck, pick up one of the books on your table and use it as a mentor!"

CONFERRING AND SMALL-GROUP WORK

If writers need support with their "about the author" page . . .

You might begin saying, "When Albert Marrin wrote an 'about the author' section to his book, *Oh, Rats*, he first told about his education and then he wrote about his relationship with his subject—rats. He wrote this about his childhood:

👏 *Rats scurried around the neighborhood of Albert's childhood home in Baltimore. He was scared of them, but gradually, as he learned more about rats, the boy lost his fear—mostly. When he saw one recently, the grown-up Dr. Marrin still got the heebie-jeebies. He lives with his wife, Yvette, in Riverdale, New York. (from* Oh, Rats! *by Albert Marrin)*

Then you could say to your students, "You could try that, too! In fact, right now, rehearse an 'about the author' section with the person sitting next to you."

If writers need support with their book blurb . . .

You could give them an example of a book blurb or small excerpts from a few book blurbs. Using the student-created book blurb chart found in the online resources, remind your writers of the key features of book blurbs—a short summary of the book so that readers know what to expect, a direct address to readers to invite them into the topic, a little story about the topic that sets the stage for what's to unfold within the

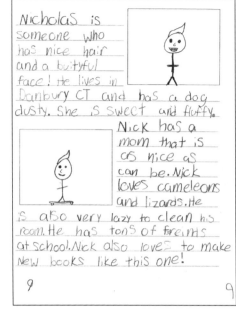

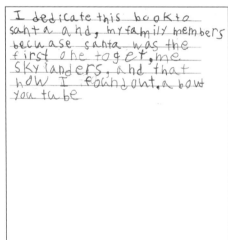

FIG. 20–1   Dedications and About the Author pages highlight the individuality of each writer.

book's covers. This time, however, share an example, perhaps from the inside cover blurb about *Oh, Rats!*, which begins with a dramatic story about rats at the start of time:

👉 *Civilization is dawning. Even then, the wily rat is unstoppable, devouring our food and earning the wrath of hungry men . . . So the story of rats and people begins.*
(*from* Oh, Rats! *by Albert Marrin*)

Again, you might invite students to rehearse with someone nearby on how their own book blurb might go.

SHARE

Once your writers have dressed up one of their books with a dedication, an "about the author" page, and a book blurb, it will be time to celebrate! There are many ways this celebration could go—a gallery walk, a symphony share, or partnerships reading their books to another partnership. However, we suggest that each writer create a display, with one part of their workspace titled, "I used to be the kind of writer who . . ." and the other part titled, "Now I am the kind of writer who . . ." Writers would then select a page from the first book they wrote and a page from the most recent book they wrote. They can set those two pages alongside each other to highlight their growth as information writers. Writers can add Post-its to the more recent page, calling viewers' attention to areas of growth. Alternatively, students might write insights like: "I used to be the kind of writer who wrote seven lines per page. Now I am the kind of writer who writes at least twelve lines per page." Or "I used to be the kind of writer who did not write a special beginning. Now I am the kind of writer who writes something special on every page."

Once the displays have been created, you'll want to give your students an audience—their own classmates or children from another class. Either way, help students glory in their hard work and the progress they have made. The pride that you see in them as they make public their progress will help to rally your students for the work ahead.

Be prepared to continue to celebrate their progress and to accept approximations. Always remember that the goal is not perfection—the goal is growth.

Cheers!
Lucy, Hareem, and Shana

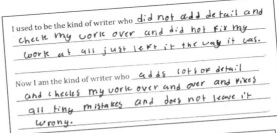

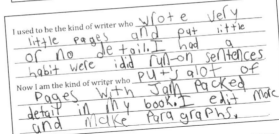

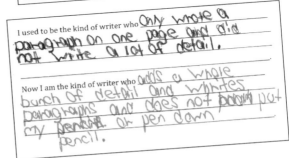

FIG. 20–2 Writers reflect and capture their insights on how they've grown.